Making the Most
of Your Field Placement

Handbook for Human Services
First Canadian Edition

Siobhan Maclean, Rob Harrison,
and
Ronda Monahan

de Sitter Publications

ACKNOWLEDGMENTS

Thanks to the following students and practitioners who contributed to this guide

- Rachel Bagnall
- Mick Baker
- Olivia Daniels
- Alison Gough
- Angela Hassall
- Joanne Kennedy
- Fran MacKay
- Terry McDermott
- Tor Meadows
- Karen Peers
- Rachel Pritchard
- Rachel Rayner
- Jane Whitfield

ABOUT THE AUTHORS

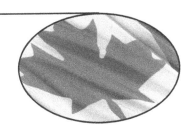

Siobhan Maclean qualified as a social worker in 1990. She has worked in a variety of settings including children's services, learning disability services and mental health services. She has been a foster caregiver, an approved social worker and a practice teacher. Siobhan now manages Kirwin Maclean Associates Limited. She acts as a researcher, trainer and consultant for a range of social care and social work organizations. Siobhan is the European Honorary Secretary for the International Federation of Social Workers.

Rob Harrison has worked in the voluntary sector since 1996. He completed his Practice Teaching Award in 2006 and has enjoyed acting as a Practice Assessor for several students, both on and off site. Rob has a particular interest in social work and practice learning in voluntary organizations and children's services, and in making theory accessible and relevant for students and practice assessors.

Ronda Monahan has a BA in Sociology and a BSW from McMasters University and a MSW from McGill University. She has taught for over 15 years in the Social Service Work, Mental Health and Addictions programs. Her clinical background includes developmental services, employment services, child welfare, forensic social work, medical social work, and more recently in crisis intervention in mental health and addictions.

Making the Most of Your Field Placement: Handbook for Human Services
First Canadian Edition

By Siobhan Maclean, Rob Harrison, and Ronda Monahan

A catalogue record for this book will be available from Library and Archives Canada

ISBN: 978-1-897160-67-1

First Edition: 2009 © Kirwin Maclean Associates Ltd
First Canadian Edition: 2014 © Kirwin Maclean Associates Ltd. /
Published by de Sitter Publications

Cover image and content pictures are licensed from fotolia.com

To order:

de Sitter Publications
111 Bell Dr., Whitby, ON, L1N 2T1
CANADA

deSitterPublications.com
289-987-0656
info@desitterpublications.com

CONTENTS

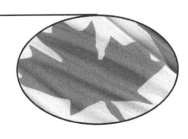

ABOUT THIS REFERENCE GUIDE

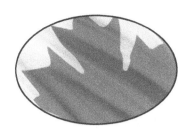

Field placement is an important training component for students entering the human service field. The human service field is composed of several different specializations including Social Service Workers (SSW), Developmental Service Workers (DSW) and Child and Youth Workers (CYW), and other related human service workers. Other related human services include specialized work in mental health, addictions gerontology, recreation and leisure, community justice and health education. Typically, field placement is the part of the program which students look forward to the most. Students can become anxious as well as excited about preparing for their field placements.

The aim of this reference guide is to support students through the field placement process, so that you are clear what steps are involved, what may be asked, how you may be assessed and evaluated, and what to do if the field placement is not working or going as planned. In addition to wanting to learn, grow, and develop, students want to come out of the field placement successfully and progress to the next stage of either their program of study or to begin their careers in the field.

Completing a field placement is not just about passing – it is critical element that links the theory covered in class to the practice required in the field. The Ministry of Training Colleges and Universities (MTCU) determine the program requirements for all college level diplomas and university degrees in Ontario. Program learning outcomes for the Social Service Worker, Developmental Service Worker, and Child and Youth Worker diplomas have been determine through a consultation process that include community stakeholders, social service agencies and the professional regulatory body that governs the registration for the field.

The Ontario College of Social Workers and Social Service Workers (OCSWSSW) is the regulatory body that all Social Workers and Social Service Workers in Ontario must register with in order to maintain their designation. The Developmental Disability Interest Group is the voluntary professional association for Developmental Service Workers and Ontario Association Child and Youth Counsellor is the voluntary professional association for Child and Youth Workers. Social service work is a professional qualification; this means that the completion of the SSW diploma permits students to apply for registration with the OCSWSSW.

This guide has been created with both sets of requirements in mind; it includes the program learning outcomes that are required by the provincial government and includes the Code of Ethics and Standards of Practice outlined by the Ontario College of Social Workers and Social Service Workers (OCSWSSW). It would be advantageous for students to download these documents as companions to this guide. While this guide is written primarily for Social Service Worker students, other programs of study that could benefit from this guide include Developmental Service Workers, Child and Youth Workers, and other related human services programs.

This reference guide is written by an experienced Faculty Advisor and has a number of sections covering some of the main issues to consider in preparing for your field placement. Students will be able to use this guide as an easy reference point at various points during field placement.

So while all college programs are governed by the provincial government, it is also important to remember that different college programs will differ in how theory and practice are integrated throughout their program of study. This guide will act as a supplement to the instruction provided by faculty supporting students in setting up meaningful field placement experiences. The reference guide is intended to support you in your learning and development as a Social Service Worker (SSW), Developmental Service Workers (DSW), Child and Youth Workers (CYW), or other related human services professionals.

A Note about Language

Throughout this book, the term "field placement" is used instead of "Professional Practice or Field Practicum" for ease of reading, although the term professional practice is important to keep in mind. Professional practice indicates the integration of theory and practice, the attainment of professional competencies and is required for professional certification/licensure. Essentially professional practice is interchangeable with practicum, field education, field work and field placement. Field Placement is about you taking every opportunity offered to put your course work into practice, and to learn from the experiences you will have throughout your field placement.

"Faculty Advisor" is another term referred to throughout this book. A number of alternative terms are used for this role – including faculty supervisor, seminar instructor or perhaps, more commonly, practice assessor. Faculty Advisor is the term that most prefer in the field. However, you should remember that your Faculty Advisor may prefer a different term. Faculty Advisors typically lead field integration seminars and evaluate student performance on placement. Faculty who are involved in matching students to practicum setting are often referred to as "Field Coordinators" or in some cases Field Preparation Faculty. "Field Liaison" is the term commonly used to identify the administrative person that supports the Field Coordinators or Faculty in setting up field placements. Many institutions have a central support person in which all documentation required for field placement is coordinated through. "Field Work Supervisor" or field supervisor is the term used to describe the role of the field placement supervisor who assigns and supervises your work onsite. Faculty Advisors and Field Work Supervisors work collaboratively with students in the field placement process.

Students are often concerned about going on placement. Anxiety and apprehension can impede learning for some students, and it can motivate and stimulates other students to work harder. This guide seeks to address these challenges so you can make the most of your learning and field placement experiences!

UNDERSTANDING THE CONTEXT OF THE FIELD PLACEMENT EXPERIENCE

This section will provide some background information about the context of field placement requirements for the SSW, DSW, and CYW diploma. It will provide some basic information on the field placement process and more importantly, the nature of relationships in the field placement agency, organization or institution. Subsequent sections provide more information and detail on the issues raised in this section.

QUALIFYING FOR A FIELD PLACEMENT

Defining the Scope of Practice

Social Service Work is governed by the Social Work and Social Service Work Act, which was introduced in 1998. A diploma in Social Service Worker is approved by the Ministry of Training Colleges and Universities and is delivered through an approved College of Applied Arts and Technology. Graduates from these approved programs are eligible to apply for registration with the Ontario College of Social Workers and Social Service Workers (OCSWSSW). The OCSWSSW is the regulatory body for both social workers and social services workers under this Act.

While the Developmental Service Workers and Child and Youth Workers are not formally governed by legislation, there is a strong movement to regulate both of these professions and this will likely occur over the next few years. The Developmental Services Worker, the Child and Youth Worker, and other related human service workers distinct professions separate from Social Service Worker, yet there are many similarities between these programs of study and consequently all of these programs of study can pathway to the Social Work profession.

What is the difference between a Social Worker and a Social Service Worker?

The scope of practice for any profession serves a regulatory function; it describes the profession's activities, outlines the boundaries for these activities, especially in relation to other professions where similar activities could be performed (OCSWSSW, 2008). The Ontario College of Social Worker and Social Service Workers (OCSWSSW) is the regulatory body that defines the roles and the scope of practice for Social Work and Social Service Workers in Ontario (MCSS, 1998). It is essential for students to understand the scope of practice of the two professions (Social Work and Social Service Worker), the distinctions between them and other human service related professions. In order to use the title of Social Worker or Social Service Worker in Ontario, you need to meet the registration requirements of the OCSWSSW, which includes the completion of educational requirements. The OCSWSSW provide definitions for each of these roles. In defining the role of Social Worker, the definition includes diagnosis and psychosocial functioning which is not within the scope of practice for the Social Service Worker (OCSWSSW, 2008).

"**Role of a social worker** means the role of a person who assesses, **diagnoses**, treats and evaluates individual, interpersonal and societal problems through the use of social work knowledge, skills, interventions and strategies, to assist individuals, dyads, families, groups, organizations and communities to achieve optimum **psychosocial** and social functioning."

"**Role of a social service** worker means the role of a person who assesses, treats and evaluates individual, interpersonal and societal problems through the use of social service work knowledge, skills, interventions and strategies, to assist individuals, dyads, families, groups, organizations and communities to achieve optimum social functioning."

Formal Training Required by the Ontario College of Social Work and Social Service Workers (OCSWSSW)

To acquire registration with OCSWSSW, students are required to complete an Ontario college diploma in Social Service Worker; similarly to acquire registration as a Social Worker; students are required to complete a Bachelor of Social Work degree, a Master of Social Work degree or a Doctorate in Social Work.

All diplomas granted by Colleges of Applied Arts and Technology (CAAT) meet the educational entrance requirements for application to the OCSWSSW. Registration with the OCSWSSW permits graduates to use the title Social Service Worker. All undergraduate or graduate degrees in Social Work from universities in Ontario meet the educational entrance requirements for application with the OCSWSSW and the subsequent use of the title Social Worker. Upon registration both groups are required to indicate to the public their registration through using the prefix RSSW (Registered Social Service Worker) or RSW (Registered Social Worker) after their name.

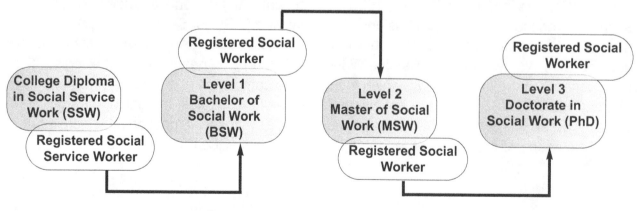

Formal Training Requirements

The formal training requirements for the Developmental Service Worker, the Child and Youth Worker, and the Social Service Worker diploma programs will be identified in this section simply because of their high affinity to the Social Work profession. Of the three diploma training requirements, Social Service Worker has the highest affinity to the Social Work profession and as a result will be covered in more depth.

Social Service Workers

Social Service Worker (SSW) programs are typically two years in length and must adhere to standards set by the provincial government. "Providing students with practical, integrated learning experiences and a body of knowledge related to the promotion of human well-being and the affirmation of strengths and capacities of people in their environments" is the aim of all SSW programs in Ontario (MTCU, 2007). The standards required of SSW graduates include: maintaining professional relationships which adhere to legal and ethical standards, a commitment to social justice, to promote the development and sustainability of a culture of equality, and to work with individuals, families, groups, and communities in identifying and mobilizing resources to facilitate opportunities for positive change (MTCU, 2007).

The following is a list of nine program learning outcomes required to complete the Social Service Work program diploma in Ontario (MTCU, 2007).

1. Develop and maintain professional relationships which adhere to professional, legal, and ethical standards aligned to social service work.
2. Identify strengths, resources, and challenges of individuals, families, groups, and communities to assist them in achieving their goals.
3. Recognize diverse needs and experiences of individuals, groups, families, and communities to promote accessible and responsive programs and services.
4. Identify current social policy, relevant legislation, and political, social, and/or economic systems and their impacts on service delivery.
5. Advocate for appropriate access to resources to assist individuals, families, groups, and communities.
6. Develop and maintain positive working relationships with colleagues, supervisors, and community partners.
7. Develop strategies and plans that lead to the promotion of self-care, improved job performance, and enhanced work relationships.
8. Integrate social group work and group facilitation skills across a wide range of environments, supporting growth and development of individuals, families, and communities.
9. Work in communities to advocate for change strategies that promote social and economic justice and challenge patterns of oppression and discrimination.

Program Standards for Social Service Worker (SSW) graduates are set by the Ministry of Training and Colleges and Universities, and can be downloaded at www.tcu.gov.on.ca/pepg/audiences/colleges/progstan/humserv/socialServ.pdf

Developmental Service Workers

The following chart details the seven program learning outcomes required to complete the Developmental Service Worker program diploma in Ontario. The chart captures the latest version of program learning outcomes that have been created as a part of the more recent call to update standards for the developmental service sector (MTCU, 2012).

1. Conduct oneself in an ethical, competent, and accountable manner in all professional relationships.
2. Provide person-directed supports and services that respect and promote self-determination for people with developmental disabilities.
3. Provide for the safety of people with developmental disabilities, self, and others in compliance with all applicable legislation, regulations, and standards of practice.
4. Support health and well-being of people with developmental disabilities.
5. Employ and adapt formal and informal strategies to support the learning of people with developmental disabilities.
6. Provide leadership in the development of inclusive communities.
7. Develop professional and personal plans that enhance job performance and well-being.

Program Standards for Developmental Service Worker (DSW) graduates are set by the Ministry of Training and Colleges and Universities, and can be found at
http://www.tcu.gov.on.ca/pepg/audiences/colleges/progstan/humserv/edevserw.pdf

Child and Youth Worker

The following chart details the eight program learning outcomes required to complete the Child and Youth Worker program diploma in Ontario.

1. Develop and maintain therapeutic relationships.
2. Foster and utilize therapeutic environments of residential and non-residential nature which respect culture, promotes well-being, and facilitates positive change for children, youth, and their families.
3. Design and implement strategies which promote client self advocacy and community education to enhance psycho social development in children, youth, and their families.
4. Employ effective intervention strategies in the areas of therapeutic programing, individual conselling and group work which comply with the treatment aims for their client.
5. Collaborate with service providers and from professional relationships in order to enhance the quality of service for children, youth, and their families.

continued...

6. Perform ongoing self assessments and utilize self care strategies to enhance professional competence.
7. Identify and use professional development resources and activities which promote professional growth.
8. Communicate effectively in oral, written, nonverbal, and electronic forms to enhance quality of service.

Program Standards for the Child and Youth Worker (CYW) graduate are set by the Ministry of Training, Colleges and Universities, and can be found at http://www.tcu.gov.on.ca/pepg/audiences/colleges/progstan/humserv/echildyt.pdf.

The course work for each of these programs of study is complemented by a supervised field placement. Each college in Ontario determines the specific program structure and curriculum, therefore, hours of field placement are not uniform across the province. Typically students in a SSW program will spend between 500 and 700 hours in field placement throughout their program (OCSWSSW, 2008). Field placement requirements in the Developmental Service Worker and other related human service programs are similar; however, field placement requirements in the Child and Youth Worker (CYW) program is different. The CYW program is an Advanced Diploma in Ontario, which is a three year college diploma with increased field placement requirements. Graduates from all three diplomas may pathway into the university level training in Social Work or other related degree programs of study.

Formal Training for Social Workers

The formal training for a Social Worker is different than a Social Service Worker. Social work programs are recognized as professional programs within the university system and are subject to external accreditation requirements.

There are three levels of university degrees offered in social work in Canada. The first university level degree for a social worker is the *Bachelor of Social Work (BSW)* degree; this is typically a four year honours degree, obtained in a university social work program. The second level university degree is a *Master of Social Work (MSW)*, a graduate degree, which includes a further one to two years of schooling which may include a field placement and a research study (thesis). While some Social Workers possess a BSW or MSW, many hold both degrees. The third level university degree is the *doctoral degree (PhD)* in Social Work that is typically geared towards research and teaching.

The aim of the Bachelor of Social Work is to "ensure that graduates will be broadly educated and prepared for general practice and have sufficient competence for an entry level Social Work position. Competence is evidenced by an ability to arrive at professional judgments and practice actions, based on integration of theory and practice within the context of professional values and the relevant Social Work Code of Ethics" (Canadian Association of Social Work Education, 2007). The box below outlines requirements at the university level for Social Work.

The Social Work level degree requires that graduates have:

- Knowledge related to human development and behaviour in the social environment.

- Critical analysis of Canadian social work, social welfare history and social policy and their implications for social work practice with diverse populations, including racial minorities.

- Beginning level analysis and practice skills pertaining to the origins and manifestations of social injustices in Canada, and the multiple and intersecting bases of oppression, domination, and exploitation.

- Practice methods and professional skills required for generalist practice (i.e., analysis of situations, establishing accountable relationships, intervening appropriately, and evaluating one's own social work interventions) at a beginning level of competence.

- Understanding of social work's origins, purposes, and practices.

- Understanding of and ability to apply social work values and ethics in order to make professional judgements consistent with a commitment to address inequality and the eradication of oppressive social conditions.

- Awareness of self in terms of values, beliefs, and expectations as these impact upon social work practice.

- Ability to undertake systematic inquiry and critical evaluation related to social work knowledge and practice.

- Knowledge of multiple theoretical and conceptual bases of social work knowledge and practice including the social construction of theory and practices that may reflect injustices.

- Knowledge of other related occupations and professions sufficient to facilitate interprofessional collaboration and team work.

- An understanding of oppressions and healing of Aboriginal peoples and implications for social policy and social work practice with Aboriginal peoples in the Canadian context.

- Opportunities to develop an appreciation of social work purposes and ethics and to develop her/his social work values and professional judgement.

- Preparation to practice in a range of geographical regions and with diverse ethnic, cultural, and racial populations.

(Canadian Association of Social Work Education, 2007)

Similar to the SSW diploma and other human service related diploma programs, the field placement is an essential component of the curriculum at the university level. Students are required to complete a minimum of 700 practice hours at the BSW level (Canadian Association of Social Work Education, 2007). MSW programs require that students complete a minimum of 450 practicum hours in one year degree programs plus an additional 450 practicum hours and/or a thesis in two year degree programs (Canadian Association of Social Work Education, 2007).

Although the objectives and curriculum for BSW and MSW programs differ, the scope of practice is the same for all Social Workers, regardless of level of education at the university level. Employers in the field differentiate between the various levels of training and education through job descriptions and pay scales.

What is the difference between Social Work knowledge and Social Service Work knowledge?

Although there is overlap in curriculum between SSW college programs and BSW university programs, there are four key differences between the bodies of knowledge at the college and university level:

	University	**College**
Intensity	University programs stress systematic inquiry, critical evaluation, analysis, and professional judgements.	College programs stress identifying strenghts, resources, challenges, and social and political issues that impact service delivery and advocate for appropriate resources.
Breadth	University programs require two additional years of study before taking social work courses. The first two years focus on building a broad general knowledge base and emphasis is placed on interconnections with bodies of knowledge in a holistic manner.	College programs are two years in length and focus on applied learning.
Theory	University programs focus on teaching students to think critically in an analytic manner.	College programs will teach some theory but students would not be expected to have the breadth of knowledge of individual theories.
Research	University programs require both statistical and research courses.	College programs do not require statistical and research courses.

The bodies of knowledge for these two distinct professions are differentiated by intensity, breadth, research and theory. The differences, though slight, are critical. These differences relate to general knowledge, depth of perception, ability to analyze, ability to critique, ability to test and to seek new knowledge. This gap of knowledge is greater for Developmental Service Worker and Child and Youth Worker.

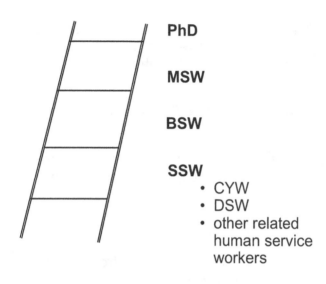

PhD

MSW

BSW

SSW
- CYW
- DSW
- other related human service workers

There are a number of university Social Work programs that will grant advanced standing to graduates with SSW diplomas. Similarly there are pathways for Developmental Service Workers, Child and Youth Workers, and other related human service workers to bridge to a university level Social Work program. In fact many colleges and universities are forming partnerships so that students can continue to develop in the profession by transitioning from college level diploma to university degree. Understanding the differences in knowledge base between college and university level training will allow students to understand how this impacts their scope of practice in the field.

So what is the difference between the Role of Social Service Worker and Social Worker?

Defining the role or the scope of practice for a profession is done by looking at what the profession does, what methods the profession uses and what is the purpose for which the profession does it (OCSWSSW, 2008). So while there is overlap between the scopes of practice between a Social Service Worker and Social Worker, there are three distinguishing factors that differentiate the two roles.

Three Distinguishing Factors that Differentiate the Role of a Social Service Worker and a Social Worker (OCSWSSW, 2008):	
1. **What the profession does**	• The scope of practice statement for social work includes the ability to conduct social work diagnosis. • The scope of practice statement for social service work does not include diagnosis.

2. Methods used by the profession	• The scope of practice statement for social work uses social work knowledge, skills, intervention, and strategies.
	• The scope of practice statement for social service work uses social work knowledge, skills, intervention and strategies.
3. The purpose for which the profession does an activity	• The scope of practice statement for social work includes as a purpose for social work activity the achievement of optimum psychosocial functioning.
	• The scope of practice statement for social service work does not include this purposes.

What the Profession Does

The scope of practice for Social Work includes "diagnosis," while the scope of practice for Social Service Work does not. Diagnosis is defined as "the series of judgements made by a social worker based on social work knowledge and skills in regard to individuals, couples, families, and groups. These judgements: a) serve as the basis of actions to be taken or not taken in a case for which the social worker has assumed professional responsibility; and b) are based on the Social Work Code of Ethics and Standards of Practice. Such judgements and the procedures and actions leading from them are matters for which the Social Worker expects to be accountable" (OCSWSSW, 2008).

A diagnosis can also be made with couples, families, and groups. When making an individual diagnosis, it is expected that a Social Worker understand the personality structure of the client as well as understand the societal realities in which the client functions. This analysis is commonly referred to as "person in environment"; moreover, focuses on the need to make an accurate formulation of "who is the client," "what is their reality," and "how do the two interface?" (OCSWSSW, 2008). This process is called the formulation of a social diagnosis and is the core of Social Work practice (Turner, 2002). This activity requires that a Social Worker make an ongoing series of judgements as to the nature of the presenting situation and based on these judgements formulate an action plan which the Social Worker will be held accountable.

The formulation of a social work diagnosis is not within the scope of practice of Social Service Work because the two years of training limit the depth and breadth of the interpersonal and social theory. Based on the theoretical and practical knowledge acquired in the Social Service Work programs at the college level, the SSW will understand that "diagnosis" is the summary of judgements on which professional action is taken. The Social Service Worker may follow a suggested course of action based on a diagnosis that was identified by another professional, but will not be required to make the social diagnosis.

Methods Used By the Profession

The methods used by Social Service Workers and Social Workers are not different in the scope of practice statement; however, there is a distinction based on formal levels of training and education which distinguishes the intensity, breadth, depth, comprehensiveness, and theoretical framework of knowledge of methods used by the Social Service Worker and Social Worker.

The Purpose for Which the Profession Does an Activity

Finally the purpose for which the profession does an activity is the final differentiator used to understand the differences between the scope of practice for Social Workers and Social Service Workers. Social Workers aim to achieve "optimum psychosocial functions," while the scope of practice for Social Service Workers does not include this.

What is implied by the term "psychosocial" is the ability of the Social Worker to not only assess the nature and functioning of the personality of the client(s), including the broad range of cultural, historic, values, strengths, potentials, and areas of stress, but also how a client interfaces with the broad spectrum of complex and interfacing societal systems. The purpose of social work interventions and strategies is to achieve optimum functioning at both the emotional, interpersonal, and social systemic levels (OCSWSSW, 2008).

Performing "psychosocial assessments" is not an expectation that can be mastered within a college level Social Service Worker program. Although Social Service Workers will understand that the social and psychological variables of a client are interrelated, they will not have obtained the depth and breadth of knowledge required to bring about changes in the psychosocial functioning of the individual.

Not all practice situations will require changes in psychosocial functioning of an individual; however, a client's psychosocial issues may create barriers to their being able to make use of services or treatment. For example, it is expected that a social service worker would be able to apply crisis intervention skills in circumstances where the goal of service is to provide support and link the client to other helping resources. The social worker, however, based on their advanced level of therapeutic knowledge and skill would also be able to assist the client in dealing with issues that result from past trauma (OCSWSSW, 2008).

The Field of Employment

The Ontario College of Social Worker and Social Service Workers has no oversight over employers, therefore, has no authority to direct or advise an employer on whether to hire a social workers or a social service workers, developmental service worker or a child and youth worker to perform specific jobs within an organization (OCSWSSW, 2008). The scope of practice is different from a job description; employers define the various roles and duties to be performed by the employees they hire. Job description typically will require a certain level of training based on the duties required and consequently salaries are often aligned to these different levels of training requirements.

How do occupations get classified in Canada?

The National Occupation Classification (NOC) is what is used to classify job descriptions by employers in Canada (HRDC, 2011). Community and Social Service Worker (NOC 4212) includes DSW, CYW, SSW, SW, and other related human service workers. Job duties include (HRDC, 2011):

- Interview clients to obtain case history and background information
- Assess clients' relevant skill strengths and deficits
- Assist clients to develop plans of action while providing necessary support and assistance
- Assist clients in finding community resources (i.e., legal, medical, financial, housing, employment, transportation, child care assistance, and other referral services).
- Prepare intake reports
- Counsel clients living in group homes and half-way houses, supervise their activities and assist in pre-release and release planning
- Participate in the selection and admission of clients to appropriate programs
- Assess and investigate eligibility for social benefits
- Meet with clients to assess their progress, give support, and discuss any difficulties or problems
- Refer clients to other social services
- Advise and aid recipients of social assistance and pensions
- Provide crisis intervention and emergency shelter services
- Implement and organize the delivery of specific services within the community
- Implement change strategies (i.e., life skills, substance abuse, behaviour management, and youth services) under the supervision of a supervisor
- Assist in evaluating the effectiveness of treatment programs by tracking clients' behavioural changes and responses to interventions
- Maintain relationships with other community agencies and health care providers involved with clients' needs and overall progress
- Co-ordinate volunteer activities of human services agencies, health care facilities, and arts and sports organizations
- Maintain program statistics for purposes of evaluation and research
- May supervise community support workers and volunteers

Code of Ethics

The values that guide the Social Service Worker profession include service, social justice, dignity, worth, the importance of human relationships, integrity, and competence. The purpose of the Code of Ethics is to set forth values and principles to guide the professional conduct of Social Service Workers and Social Workers. While a code of ethics cannot guarantee ethical behaviour, it guides the professions as they act in good faith and with a genuine desire to make sound decisions (OCSWSSW, 2008).

Code of Ethics and Standards of Practice for Social Work and Social Service Workers (2008)

1. A social worker or social service worker shall maintain the best interest of the client as the primary professional obligation;

2. A social worker or social service worker shall respect the intrinsic worth of the persons she or he serves in her or his professional relationships with them;

3. A social worker or social service worker shall carry out her or his professional duties and obligations with integrity and objectivity;

4. A social worker or social service worker shall have and maintain competence in the provision of a social work or social service work service to the client;

5. A social worker or social service worker shall not exploit the relationship with a client for personal benefit, gain or gratification;

6. A social worker or social service worker shall protect the confidentiality of all professionally acquired information. He or she shall disclose such information only when required or allowed by law to do so, or when clients have consented to disclosure;

7. A social worker or social service worker who engages in another profession, occupation, affiliation or calling shall not allow these outside interests to affect the social work or social service work relationship with the client;

8. A social worker or social service worker shall not provide social work or social service work services in a manner that discredits the profession of social work or social service work or diminishes the public's trust in either profession;

9. A social worker or social service worker shall advocate for workplace conditions and policies that are consistent with this Code of Ethics and the Standards of Practice of the Ontario College of Social Workers and Social Service Workers;

10. A social worker or a social service worker shall promote excellence in his or her respective profession;

11. A social worker or social service worker shall advocate change in the best interest of the client, and for the overall benefit of society, the environment, and the global community.

The Code of Ethics and Standards of Practice is a requirement expected for everyone working as a registered Social Service Worker or Social Worker. As such, all Field Work Supervisors, Faculty Advisors and students should work in line with the codes of ethics and should have a copy. The Code of Ethics and Standards of Practice is available online at www.ocswssw.org.

Similarly, Child and Youth Workers have a professional association with an established mission, objectives, and a Code of Ethics for the Child and Youth Counsellor Profession. The Ontario Association of Child and Youth Counsellors is the professional body that has created a Code of Ethics for Child and Youth Workers (Counsellors) and is available on line at www.oacyc.org.

Code of Ethics for the Child and Youth Counsellor profession (OACYC, 2010)

1. We will treat client/family with dignity and will respect their unique differences in culture, religion, race, and sexual orientation.
2. We will respect the confidentiality of each client/family.
3. We will respect, safeguard, and advocate for the rights of each client and/or family.
4. We will be knowledgeable about and adhere to all relevant municipal, provincial, and federal laws.
5. We will not use or condone the use of corporal punishment under any circumstances.
6. We will not condone sexual involvement with clients.
7. We will develop, implement, and administer the policies and procedures of our respective agencies and institutions.
8. We will only enter into contracts that allow us to maintain our professional integrity.
9. We will cooperate with other professions which offer service to our clientele.
10. Recognizing that we are a catalyst for change we will:
    a) utilize current and knowledgeable methods and techniques in order to provide quality service to our clientele and;
    b) actively seek out opportunities to learn and develop as well as support growth in our co-workers and other professionals.
11. We will promote client autonomy and increased self-esteem.
12. We will treat our client holistically, encompassing family, peer group, and community.
13. We are committed to the ongoing development of our profession through competent training and supervision of Child and Youth Worker students.
14. We will conduct ourselves in a professional and ethical manner at all times.

Code of Ethics and Standards of Practice for the Developmental Service Worker (DSSIG, 2011)

Standard 1: Provision of Services to Service Recipients

DSWs adhere to the following principles during service provision:

- DSWs use a person-centred approach in the provision of services
- DSWs respect and facilitate self-determination
- DSWs ensure that an individual is provided with complete information in a format which s/he understands when making decisions
- DSWs and service recipients work together to set and evaluate goals
- DSWs utilize all possible methodologies to support individuals to communicate effectively
- DSWs ensure that each service recipient's human rights are maintained
- DSWs provide competent professional services to all individuals, irrespective of gender, race, religion, sexual orientation, age or ability

Standard 2: Competence

- DSWs have a unique body of knowledge.
- DSWs engage in professional practice.
- DSWs are committed to ongoing professional learning.
- DSWs have a specific scope of practice.

Standard 3: Integrity

- Because they support individuals with developmental disabilities, DSWs are in a position of power with respect to these individuals. DSWs ensure that the service recipients whom they support are protected from abuse of this power.

continued...

Standard 4: Confidentiality

- DSWs maintain the privacy of individuals they support.

Standard 5: Consent

- DSWs uphold the legal rights of a service recipient to give voluntary and informed consent to release of information in any format or to receipt of services.

Standard 6: Fees

- DSWs exercise professional behaviour and follow legal requirements when setting or collecting fees from service recipients or designates.

The Developmental Services Special Interest Group is the professional association that represents DSWs in Ontario. The DSW Standards of Practice is available online at www.oadd.org/

If people involved in the provision of your field placement are working from different codes or standards of practice such as those noted above, it is a useful exercise to compare and contrast the different codes of ethics and/or standards of practice to enhance your learning.

Learning Activities

To meet requirements set out by provincial government you need to have a range of learning activities during your field placement. These typically include carrying a small caseload, shadowing experienced workers, attending relevant meetings and visiting a range of allied services. However, this is not an exhaustive list and the opportunities available within a given placement will be identified within each agency, organization or institution before you are offered a field placement. It should be emphasized that you are expected to undertake direct work with people who use services; observing experienced workers is an important way to learn, but is not sufficient to meet the requirements.

Diversity in field placement settings

SSW, DSW, CYW, and other related human service students may do their field placement in a diverse range of settings. These include federal, provincial, and municipal governments; group homes; shelters; community centres; programs for the physically and developmentally challenged; mental health services; child protection agencies; addictions facilities, older adult services, and educational and long term health care settings – the list of potential placements is endless. By having a diverse range of settings you will have the opportunity to have to experience many different learning activities. This guide has been created to ensure that you maximize each opportunity and identify the learning which can be transferred from the whole range of possible placements.

What makes a good field placement?

There is plenty of research to support that there are many factors related to having a positive experience on field placement. Bogo (2010) found that students report higher satisfaction with their field placements when the Field Work Supervisor and student relationship was perceived to be of high quality (Bogo, M., 2010). Similarly, Drolet and Clark (2012) suggest that the quality of field placement instruction is primarily based on the Field Work Supervisor and student relationship as well as the range of learning activities (Drolet & Clark, 2012). The quality of the Field Work Supervisor and student relationship impacts student success (Fortune, McCarthy, & J.Abramson, 2001). In addition, students have indicated other important factors that are associated with a successful field placement.

It makes sense that when students feel supported by their Field Work Supervisors, when they have meaningful learning activities, when they have opportunities to reflection and integrate theory and practice and when the placement setting that is aligned with the values of their profession and is supportive of having student's onsite; all of these factors lead to a successful field placement. Given there is some consensus on the importance of the factors, it is concerning that students often report dissatisfaction with their field placements.

This guide aims to give you an overview of how to make sure that your field placement works for you, no matter where you are placed.

SUMMARY

The educational requirements for Social Service Worker, Child and Youth Workers, and Developmental Service Workers are at the diploma level in Ontario. Students will spend a minimum between 500-700 hours in field placement as part of their training. Field placements offer you the opportunity to demonstrate your skills and abilities as a professional and develop your confidence across a range of settings within which you will be employed. This guide will help you to make the most of the opportunities provided to you on your field placement.

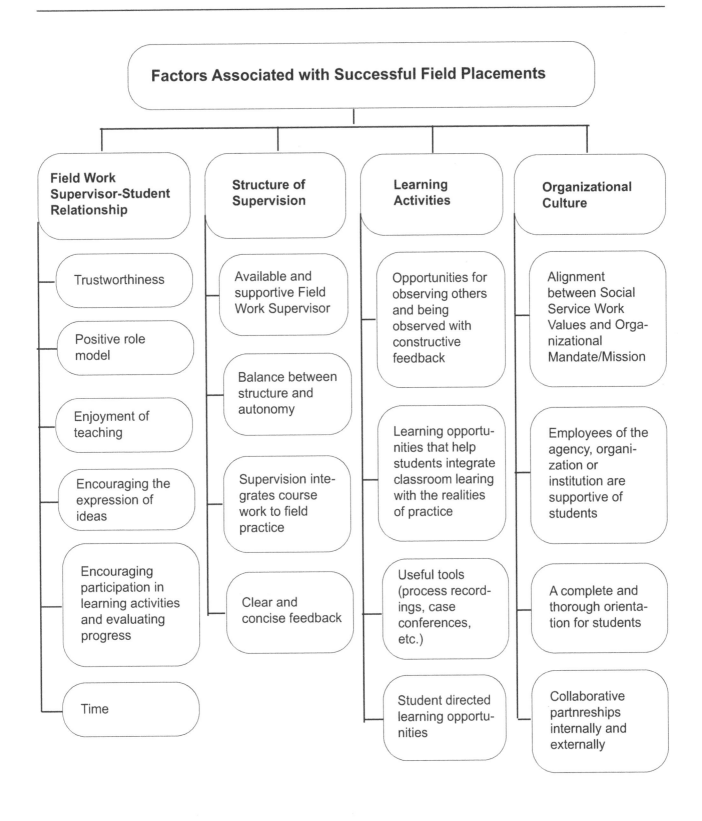

Factors Associated with Successful Field Placements

Field Work Supervisor-Student Relationship

- Trustworthiness
- Positive role model
- Enjoyment of teaching
- Encouraging the expression of ideas
- Encouraging participation in learning activities and evaluating progress
- Time

Structure of Supervision

- Available and supportive Field Work Supervisor
- Balance between structure and autonomy
- Supervision integrates course work to field practice
- Clear and concise feedback

Learning Activities

- Opportunities for observing others and being observed with constructive feedback
- Learning opportunities that help students integrate classroom learing with the realities of practice
- Useful tools (process recordings, case conferences, etc.)
- Student directed learning opportunities

Organizational Culture

- Alignment between Social Service Work Values and Organizational Mandate/Mission
- Employees of the agency, organization or institution are supportive of students
- A complete and thorough orientation for students
- Collaborative partnreships internally and externally

THE FIELD PLACEMENT PROCESS

2

While it is important to remember that each program will differ in terms of requirements (e.g., number of days spent in field placement during an academic year, and documentation requirements), field placements generally follow a similar process for all diploma level programs in Ontario. The field placement process diagram on the following page can be helpful in giving you an outline of the stages which your placement is likely to follow.

This chapter gives a brief outline of each stage of the process. More detail on specific areas is given in the remaining sections of the guide.

Professional Development Portfolio

Most programs of study provide a set of guidelines for developing a professional development portfolio to students in their field preparation course. Professional development portfolios or educational portfolios can be organized in various ways. Given that all college programs in Ontario are guided by programs learning outcomes, some colleges require that students submit evidence of their competence with a professional development portfolio using these program learning outcomes. In other cases, students may choose to organize their portfolio around courses they have taken, submitting course outlines, papers, exams, evaluations, and other materials. Finally others may choose to organize their portfolios around themes such as knowledge, skills, values, philosophy of helping, and goals for professional development (Myers Kiser, 2008).

While not all programs of study use the professional development portfolio in the field placement process, the majority of colleges require students to provide evidence of their work at the completion of the program. Many programs introduce the concept of the profession development portfolio early in the program of study and have students work on this throughout their entire program. The professional development portfolio is an effective tool used to demonstrate that you have met the program requirements and it can also be a real employment advantage upon graduation when you use it as part of your job search (Baird, 1999).

Field Placement Requests

Some programs of study may not use the professional development portfolio and instead have students submit a field placement request form which may also be referred to as a personal profile. In some cases, a field placement request, a professional development portfolio, and a resume may be requested by Field Coordinator, Field Preparation Faculty

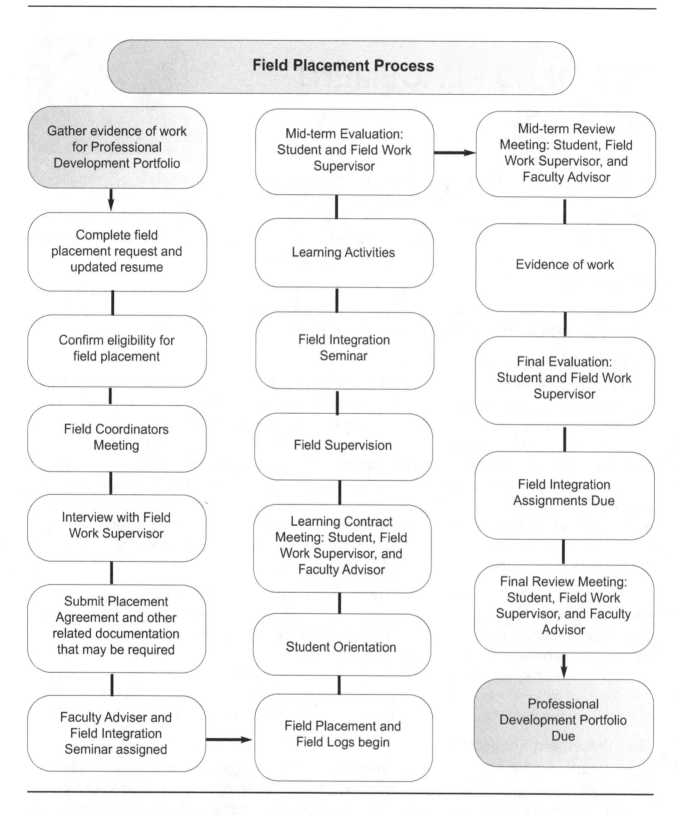

Field Placement Process

Gather evidence of work for Professional Development Portfolio

Complete field placement request and updated resume

Confirm eligibility for field placement

Field Coordinators Meeting

Interview with Field Work Supervisor

Submit Placement Agreement and other related documentation that may be required

Faculty Adviser and Field Integration Seminar assigned

Mid-term Evaluation: Student and Field Work Supervisor

Learning Activities

Field Integration Seminar

Field Supervision

Learning Contract Meeting: Student, Field Work Supervisor, and Faculty Advisor

Student Orientation

Field Placement and Field Logs begin

Mid-term Review Meeting: Student, Field Work Supervisor, and Faculty Advisor

Evidence of work

Final Evaluation: Student and Field Work Supervisor

Field Integration Assignments Due

Final Review Meeting: Student, Field Work Supervisor, and Faculty Advisor

Professional Development Portfolio Due

Note: It is important to remember that programs vary in terms of requirements. The process may therefore need to be adapted depending on particular requirements.

and or the Field Liaison involved in setting up your placements. At times, students do not always recognize the importance of completing these forms or in compiling this information. This information will be used by the Field Coordinator to make a field placement match. Eligibility for field placement is determined by the Program Coordinator and it is typically reviewed once the placement request is submitted. Many colleges require specific course work to be completed prior to being approved to going out on field placement.

Often the placement request forms and resumes are sent out to agencies, organizations, and institutions for Field Work Supervisors to review. Field Work Supervisors may receive a number of placement requests and make a decision about which student to offer a placement to, based on what is submitted. So you must not underestimate the importance of the field placement request, the resume, the cover letter and the professional development portfolio in the screening process.

Field Coordinator Meeting

Many programs require that students attend a meeting with faculty who are involved with matching students to practicum sites. You will be expected to submit your cover letter, resume, and placement request to field preparation faculty beforehand. During this meeting, you may be expected to bring their current professional development portfolio or other relevant materials to support the process of matching field placement. Your eligibility for placement will be confirmed and possible practicum sites will be explored. You will be matched to a practicum site based on the programs criteria for field placement matching. Each program will have its own set criteria for matching students to practicum sites, this criteria is typically covered in your field preparation seminars. Student preference, student readiness, academic performance, previous experience in the human service field, employment history, volunteer experience, and letters of recommendations are some of the possible criteria used to match students. Students are expected to set up interviews with potential Field Work Supervisors once an agency, organization or institution has been recommended.

Interview with Field Work Supervisor

Many practicum sites require students to attend an interview as part of their selection process. Other agencies, organizations or institutions make their selection based on the students resume, cover letter, and placement request form. At the interview, the Field Work Supervisor will ask a series of questions to determine suitability for field placement. You may present your professional development portfolio at the interview. It is important to discuss expectations and opportunities with the Field Work Supervisor and staff. The staff and Field Work Supervisor will want to know more about you and your needs, so you will need to be well prepared for this interview. It is critical that you make a positive first impression at the onset as this can set the tone for the entire field placement. This meeting should be arranged by you and it is important that you are prepared.

At this point, if you or your Field Work Supervisors feel that there are potential difficulties which cannot be addressed, the placement opportunity may not go ahead.

Preparing for this interview

You may want to do research on the agency, organization or institution prior to attending the interview. It is important to research websites or consult community directories to gain a better understanding of what the agency, organization or institution does and who they serve in the community. Preparing a list of questions is a good idea. Having a list ready prior to the interview is a good way of ensuring that you will have a successful interview. The list could include:

- What ground rules are likely to apply to you around issues such as dress and use of cell phones? Lots of students ask about dress and what will be expected in terms of their appearance, and it can be helpful to clarify your Field Work Supervisor's opinions on exactly what casual means to them, or to look at what colleagues wear when you visit. This can avoid dress becoming an issue for either you or anyone else while you are on placement. More details around ground rules and these boundaries will be covered later in this guide.

- What hours of work are expected and what time should you arrive there on your first day?

- What do you do in the event that there is an emergency or if you are ill.

- Parking – this can often be a challenge in many practicum sites!

- Consideration of what precisely YOU need to know about the role, the workload, the staff, the wider organization, the learning activities, or the expectations of the placement. Again a list can be helpful and it will show that you have given prior thought to this meeting.

- What information does the Field Work Supervisor need to know about you in relation to the field placement? (see Chapter 11 for more details.)

Placement Agreement and Other Required Documents

All programs require some form of placement/workplace agreement between the educational institution and the agency, organization or institution. The Work/Education Placement Agreement for Post-Secondary form is used by colleges and universities in Ontario and is to be completed prior to placement start-up. The placement agreement details college liability insurance for students. (It will identify hours of work, location, Field Work Supervisor's name and contact information.)

Some agencies, organizations, and institutions require medical clearance and criminal reference check to be completed prior to beginning field placement. Failing to complete this documentation will prevent you from beginning their field placement. Once this documentation is submitted a Field Placement Manual is typically sent to the practicum site. Most Field Placement Manuals detail the roles and responsibilities of all parties involved. It will also include mid-term and final evaluations used as well as identify important dates to remember during field placement. Once placements have been confirmed, the Field Coordinator will forward this to the Field Work Supervisor. Confirmation of the field placements is usually done when the Work/Education Placement Agreement for Post-Secondary form is signed by all parties. A sample of the Work/Education Placement Agreement for Post-Secondary is available at:http://www.forms.ssb.gov.on.

Field Integration Seminar

While in placement, most colleges require that students attend a Field Integration Seminar onsite, or participate in an online Field Integrative Seminar. This purpose of this seminar is to support students in being able to link their learning from the classroom to their practice in the field. Before field placement begins, you will be assigned to a Faculty Advisor. Faculty Advisors attend meetings at practicum sites, evaluate your performance, and typically teach/lead Field Integration Seminars.

Student Orientation

Generally, you will need to know about your agencies, organizations or institutions mission statement, objectives, standards, and policies at the beginning of field placement. As part of your orientation you need to learn about the practices of the agency, organization or institution (e.g., signing in and out, health and safety policies, and operational procedures). You will also likely meet key people, observe experienced workers, and begin to develop a sense of your role within the agency, organization or institution.

It is likely that your agency, organization or institution will have an existing orientation package and possibly a standard orientation program for you to attend. It is important that you be engaged at your orientation. You know the importance of first impressions – and your orientation period will be the time when most of the people you will be working with will meet you for the first time. Some Field Work Supervisors encourage students to be proactive in their orientation, for example, by providing a list of contacts and asking students to arrange their own visits. This can be an excellent way of helping you to orientate yourself to the field placement agency, organization or institution.

Learning Contract Meeting

Once it is agreed that the placement will go ahead, a formal meeting will take place. This is sometimes referred to as a pre-placement meeting, a learning contract/agreement meeting. At this meeting a learning contract, is drawn up. You are expected to come prepared to this meeting with a rough draft of your learning contract. This meeting formalizes arrangements and identifies your goals and objectives for the field placement. The meeting is attended by you, your Field Work Supervisor and your Faculty Advisor. This meeting is a further opportunity for potential difficulties within your placement to be identified and avoided if possible.

This meeting may take place before you actually start your placement; however, it is typically scheduled within the first week or two of the field placement. It is important that it is no later than this since the learning contract is a key document in ensuring that every person is aware of your specific goals and objective and the roles and responsibilities of everyone involved.

Ensure that you make full use of the meeting and the negotiation of the learning contract to clarify any concerns or confusion and to establish positive communication. What is expected of you will be made clear – take the opportunity to clarify what you expect of others. All of this should be covered in this initial meeting to ensure your placement starts off positively.

What may be expect by you at this meetings

- Clear expectations around the hours you will be expected to work while on field placement and some idea of the workload you will be expected to carry.

- Clear lines of accountability for your practice and how your work will be evaluated.

- Discussion around how learning activities will be provided to meet your identified learning goals and objectives and the key roles and responsibilities, which will be assessed and evaluated.

- Respect for you as an individual and for your prior knowledge and experience.

- Positive working relationships to be established by all parties involved in the field placement process.

- Documentation provided by your program (e.g., learning contract format) is worked through and expectations around learning goals, objectives, activities, and methods of evaluation. When and what will be required at review meetings should be made clear to everyone.

What is likely to be expected of you at this meeting

- Preparation around your individual learning goals and objectives (see Chapter 11 for more detail).

- Punctuality and commitment to the process.

- Demonstration of knowledge from your course work (e.g., social welfare, social service work practice, ethics, and values).

- Respect for others' knowledge and experience.

- Enthusiasm – a list of questions and some background research into the agency, organization or institution and the placement is always a good way of showing this.

- Your Faculty Advisor and others who may be involved in setting up the placement (e.g., team leader or manager) will want to see that you are able to form positive working relationships with staff, and they are likely to expect to see you be proactive and take the initiative for building these links early on. Top tips could include smiling when you meet people and remembering and using your colleagues' names!

Learning Contract

Sometimes referred to as a placement agreement or learning contract, these are key documents in field placement. Most programs provide a set process for completion. It is important that this document be completed thoroughly following negotiation at the Learning Contract meeting. It is likely to contain:

- Practical information: including contact details, dates, and deadlines
- Information on your learning goals and objectives
- Details about learning opportunities or learning activities to be provided
- Information about how goals and objectives will be assessed and evaluated
- Information about roles and responsibilities including what field supervision arrangements will be made
- Information about expectations of all involved
- Reference to procedures to be followed, for example, in the event of concerns

You will need to make sure that everyone involved in negotiating the learning contract signs it and that you all have a copy. In the event that you (or anyone else) have concerns about the placement, this will be the key document referred to, so do make sure it is completed fully. Field Work Supervisors and Faculty Advisors will ask you to complete the contract and edit or revise any additions that result from the meeting. Whatever the arrangements for actually filling in the contract, make sure that you complete your part. Be clear about what you are "signing up for" and refer back to the contract regularly – you want to ensure that you are fulfilling your side of the contract. A sample learning contract is provided on the following page.

Social Service Worker Learning Contract

The evaluation process will vary from college to college. The evaluation process for field placement typically includes a review of the learning contract and the completion of an evaluation during the middle and final point of the field placement. You will complete the first draft of the learning contract and this will be finalized when you consult with your Field Work Supervisor. You may use the program learning outcomes for your program of study as a guide to create a draft of your learning contract. When all parties are in agreement with the learning contract, it is gets signed by you, your Field Work Supervisor, and your Faculty Advisor. The goals of the learning contract can be revised if all parties are in agreement. The sample learning contract provided is aligned to the required program learning outcomes for SSW, similar contracts can be created for DSW, CYW, and other human service related programs. Essentially the learning contract, the mid-term and final evaluations are how you will be evaluated at your field placement.

Sample Learning Contract for SSW Field Placement

Student name and contact information:		Agency/organization					
Faculty Advisor		Agency address					
Field Work Supervisor and contact information		Practicum start date					
Date learning contract received		Expected date of mid-point and final evaluation review					
Length of placement:	Days of the week at placement (FULL DAYS)	MON	TUES	WED	THURS	FRI	SAT	SUN
Projected start date:		Total hours at placement per week:					
Projected end date:		Supervision time negotiated (per week)					

Field Work Supervisors please list any expectations you may have of students in making preparation for supervision (e.g., setting the agenda, process recording, questions, oral discussion of projects, and feedback from other staff, job shadowing reports, and observations):

SSW PROGRAM LEARNING OUTCOME	LEARNING GOALS & OBJECTIVES	LEARNING ACTIVITIES	EVALUATION CRITERIA
• Develop and maintain professional relationships which adhere to professional, legal, and ethical standards aligned to social service work • Identify strengths, resources and challenges of individuals, families, groups, and communities and assist them in achieving their goals • Recognize diverse needs and experiences of individuals, groups, families, and communities to promote accessible and responsive programs and services • Identify current social policy, relevant legislation, and political, cultural and/or economic systems and their impacts on service delivery • Advocate for appropriate access to resources to assist individuals, families, groups, and communities • Develop and maintain positive working relationships with colleagues, supervisors, and community partners	• Goals and objectives are negotiated by you and your Field Work Supervisor. The Learning outcomes identified to the left may be used to assist you in the creation of goals and objectives. Goals and objectives should be specific and relevant to the context of the practicum site.	• Explains what activities you will do to demonstrate that you have met the goals and objectives. List how each goal will be achieved by detailing tasks, activities, and projects you will do.	• Explain how you will be evaluated. It is important for you to understand what the successful completion of a goal would look like.

continued...

SSW PROGRAM LEARNING OUTCOME	LEARNING GOALS & OBJECTIVES	LEARNING ACTIVITIES	EVALUATION CRITERIA
• Develop strategies and plans that lead to the promotion of self-care, improved job perform-ance and enhanced work relationships • Integrate social group work and group facilita-tion skills across a wide range of environments, supporting growth and development of individ-uals, families, and communities • Work in communities to advocate for change strategies that promote social and economic justice and challenge patterns of oppression and discrimination.			

Field Work Signature		Date	
Student Signature		Date	
Faculty Advisor Signature		Date	

Field Supervision

Once you have started your placement, supervision arrangements should be established. You will work in partnership with your Field Work Supervisor to draw up a supervision agreement and possibly a supervision "timetable." (For example, many Field Work Supervisors like to arrange supervision sessions on a set morning or afternoon each week.) Some students will include supervision arrangements in their learning contract; others may set up a separate supervision agreement. See Section E for more information on supervision. Most programs have specific requirements around time allocated to field supervision. The majority of programs require a minimum of 60 to 90 minutes per week.

Learning Activities

The Field Work Supervisor and other staff may support you in identifying learning activities for field placement. The style of these can vary, but essentially they help you to identify what learning activities you will have and who is responsible for providing these experiences. Many Field Work Supervisors will incorporate these learning activities into the learning contract negotiated at the onset. The learning contract may need to be revised as new opportunities are presented at the practicum site. It is important that a process be in place to identify these opportunities and activities whether through a learning plan or through the learning contract. The sample of learning activities below aligns to the program learning outcomes for SSW. This list may be helpful to you in identifying possible learning activities to include in your learning contract.

You should be provided with a wide range of learning opportunities. Take an active approach and engage fully in the activities provided. Engaging in these activities is imperative to you being able to gather evidence of your skills and abilities on your field placement. More information is provided in Chapter 17.

Sample of Learning Activities for the Learning Contract

Develop and maintain professional relationships which adhere to professional, legal, and ethical standards aligned to social service work

- Develop and implement a self-orientation plan
- Shadow staff/Field Work Supervison; attend staff meetings and case conferences
- Review agency organizational chart; discuss ethical dilemmas with Field Work Supervisor

continued...

Identify strengths, resources, and challenges of individuals, families, groups, and communities to assist them in achieving their goals

- Work collaboratively with clients to establish clear objectives using the strengths perspective
- Create an Eco Map; complete a client assessment
- Attend professional development opportunities to improve clinical skills

Recognize diverse needs and experiences of individuals, groups, families, and communities to promote accessible and responsive programs and services

- Take minutes, present report, etc.
- Review different types of interventions (and their purposes)
- Implement plans, locate appropriate community resources; participate in fundraising activities

Identify current social policy, relevant legislation, and political, social, and/or economic systems and their impacts on service delivery

- Apply the OCSWSSW Code of Ethics and Standards of Practice to your field work
- Ensure confidentiality of material and obtain consent to share confidential material where appropriate
- Read pertinent legislation, regulations, and policies related to the population you serve

Advocate for appropriate access to resources to assist individuals, families, groups, and communities

- Complete a community asset map
- Create list or resource binder or "community partners"; review community resource information
- Use networking list to do initial scan of services and report

Develop and maintain positive working relationships with colleagues, supervisors, and community partners

- Critique your own performance
- Use staff for consultation in an appropriate manner
- Initiate discussions with Field Work Supervisor regarding agency policies and procedures related to professional behaviour

continued...

Develop strategies and plans that lead to the promotion of self-care, improved job performance, and enhanced work relationships

- Make effective use of supervision; develop an agenda for supervision; discuss personal and professional growth as it relates to the application of social service work skills and knowledge
- Recognize how one's own social identity, location, and values can impinge on one's work with client, families, and community groups
- Log activities in order to monitor personal strengths and areas for improvement as well as agency strengths and service gaps

Integrate social group work and group facilitation skills across a wide range of environments, supporting growth and development of individuals, families, and communities

- Co-facilitate psycho educational life skills groups
- Identify environmental and community conditions which facilitate or prevent empowerment
- Integrate field learning about social justice into academic papers and discuss in integration seminar

Work in communities to advocate for change strategies that promote social and economic justice and challenge patterns of oppression and discrimination

- Recognize and address the needs of clients in relation to factors such as gender, age, race, class, religion, ability, sexual orientation, and authority position
- Identify systemic barriers and opportunities in the social environment experienced by the client system you service
- Discuss the implication of social and economic forces on their proposed intervention with client systems

Mid-term Evaluation

As the placement proceeds, you and your Field Work Supervisor will ensure that opportunities are available for you to gather evidence of your competence as it relates to the program learning outcomes for your program. Meeting the SSW program learning outcomes allows graduates to meet the educational requirements for professional registration with the OCSWSSW. Similarly, meeting the DSW program outcomes allows for registration with DSSIG and meeting the CYW program outcomes allows for registration with OACYC. See Section F for more information about providing evidence of your work.

Not all students are able to meet the requirements of field placement. If this happens to you and your Field Work Supervisor feels you are not being successful, then they should contact your Faculty Advisor immediately to arrange a meeting. Different program have different procedures for dealing with failing or marginal students.

Mid-term Review Meeting

The mid-term review is a formal meeting involving you, your Faculty Advisor, Field Work Supervisor and other supervisors (where relevant). It is essentially an opportunity to review your performance at the field placement. Some college require mid-term evaluations or progress reports at this stage. This meeting is typically led by the student and it is the student who would typically set the agenda for the discussion.

Students are typically required to provide a progress report in relation to the learning contract. Many students are required to provide evidence of their work in relation to their learning goals/objectives prior to the meeting. Both Field Work Supervisor and Faculty Advisor provide feedback on the student's ability to link course work with field placement practice. In addition to the progress report, a mid-term evaluation is completed to identify your strengths, consider any difficulties and come to an agreement on the focus of the remainder of your placement. Samples of a SSW mid-term and final evaluation are provided on the next page. Nothing which is said at this meeting should come as a surprise to you. The supervision sessions between you and your Field Work Supervisor leading up to mid-term review is likely when feedback and drafts of any evaluations will be shared with you.

Final Evaluation

The Field Work Supervisor is responsible for completing the final field placement evaluation and making recommendations of pass or fail. You will be required to self-asses your performance on field placement using a final evaluation or through writing a final reflection. The Faculty Advisor is responsible for the final grade submission and will take the recommendations made by Field Work Supervisor into account. This evaluation should be completed prior to the final review meeting. The professional development portfolio should include all evaluations of your field placement.

Sample Mid-term/Final Field Placement Evaluation for SSW

1. Develop and maintain professional relationships which adhere to professional, legal, and ethical standards aligned to social service work.				
Evidence of Performance	Yes	No	In Progress	NA
a. recognize the legislative framework governing social service work and take into account the implications for professional responsibility and accountability				

continued...

	Yes	No	In Progress	NA
b. establish working relationships that adhere to professional standards, codes of ethics, relevant legislation, and agency guidelines				
c. promote individual's strengths and right to self-determination when engaging in processes of collaboration, consultation, and advocacy				
d. use skills, such as, but not limited to, active listening; validating; reframing; confrontation; clarifying; and empathizing, to build and strengthen professional relationships in face-to-face, telephone, and electronic communication situations				
e. establish and maintain clear and appropriate boundaries between personal and professional relationships, in accordance with professional, legal, and ethical standards of practice				
f. maintain privacy of individuals and confidentiality of information, in accordance with professional, legal, and ethical standards of practice and organizational requirements				
g. recognize the impact of governance on professional relationships				
2. Identify strengths, resources, and challenges of individuals, families, groups, and communities to assist them in achieving their goals.				
Evidence of Performance	Yes	No	In Progress	NA
a. facilitate and advocate for appropriate access and referral to a continuum of formal and informal services and resources to support individual goals				
b. work collaboratively with individuals, families, groups, and communities to set and achieve goals, utilizing a holistic strengths-based approach				
c. produce written and electronic documentation which describes facts, observations, and recommendations, in accordance with legal, ethical, and professional standards, and agency protocols				
d. recognize and affirm natural support systems and networks within communities as a vehicle to facilitate positive change				
e. assist individuals in accessing community resources such as supportive counselling, group work, and community work as appropriate to their needs and goals				

continued...

3. Recognize diverse needs and experiences of individuals, groups, families, and communities to promote accessible and responsive programs and services.				
Evidence of Performance	Yes	No	In Progress	NA
a. develop effective helping relationships, identifying integration of variables such as ethnicity, age, ability, developmental stage, race, religion, gender, sexual orientation, social and economic class, and family structure b. determine biological, sociological, economic, political, environmental, spiritual, cultural, and psychosocial variables that affect human development and behaviour c. contribute to collaborative plans of action within the changing demographics, social, political, and economic composition of the community, through the use of advocacy and consultation tools and strategies d. recognize the history, culture, traditions, norms, and values of individuals and their communities to promote the development of responsive programs and services				
4. Identify current social policy, relevant legislation, and political, social, and/or economic systems and their impacts on service delivery.				
Evidence of Performance	Yes	No	In Progress	NA
a. use a structural analysis process that identifies underlying social structures to describe issues affecting individuals, families, groups, and communities b. describe the impact of relevant legislation, mandated policies, and regulations on service delivery c. review social welfare system policy initiatives from government funding bodies and service delivery organizations, and identify the effects of major policy shifts on service delivery d. identify presenting challenges of individuals, groups, families, and communities in the context of larger structural issues e. describe social problems such as violence, poverty, homelessness, mental illness, and addictions within a larger social, political, and economic context				

continued...

5. Advocate for appropriate access to resources to assist individuals, families, groups, and communities.				
Evidence of Performance	Yes	No	In Progress	NA
a. use major helping systems such as natural support, mental health, social assistance, community information, and justice systems to support individuals, groups, and families in the achievement of their goals b. identify and utilize informal helping networks and other individual resources in the creation of action plans c. identify and link with relevant community resources to facilitate referrals and to meet individual goals d. advocate with individuals, families, and groups, through effective communication and the use of technology, to problem solve, access current resources, and address gaps in service				

6. Develop and maintain positive working relationships with colleagues, supervisors, and community partners.				
Evidence of Performance	Yes	No	In Progress	NA
a. work collaboratively as a member of a team, program partnership, and/or multidisciplinary group b. consult and collaborate with relevant partners to ensure an integrated understanding of the individual's situation and to improve quality of community resources and services c. maintain accountability to colleagues, peers, and supervisors while working collaboratively and independently as required d. utilize effective problem-solving and conflict-resolution strategies within service delivery systems				

7. Develop strategies and plans that lead to the promotion of self-care, improved job performance, and enhanced work relationships.				
Evidence of Performance	Yes	No	In Progress	NA
a) seek and utilize ongoing formal and informal supervision as required				

continued...

b. seek and utilize support and feedback, related to one's own performance, strengths, challenges, and limitations, from colleagues, peers, supervisors, and other professionals as appropriate c. employ effective self-care techniques and secure appropriate support and resources as required d. develop awareness of self in terms of values, beliefs, and experiences and determine how this impacts upon the development of professional relationships with individuals, colleagues, and supervisors e. identify tools and processes for engaging in reflective practice and critical inquiry				

8. Integrate social group work and group facilitation skills across a wide range of environments, supporting growth and development of individuals, families, and communities.				

Evidence of Performance	Yes	No	In Progress	NA
a. integrate theoretical and practice models of group work pertaining to social service work				
b. utilize group facilitation strategies to promote change and address needs of group participants				
c. develop effective group leadership skills to facilitate and address the needs and strengths of diverse groups				
d. research, plan, evaluate, and develop proposals and strategies to establish new groups				
e. monitor and facilitate group process and implement appropriate interventions and group-building strategies				

9. Work in communities to advocate for change strategies that promote social and economic justice and challenge patterns of oppression and discrimination.				

Evidence of Performance	Yes	No	In Progress	NA
a. identify and use community development models to determine community needs, risks, and assets and to promote positive social change				
b. contribute to action plans, funding proposals, and community capacity building and assessment strategies to influence and promote positive social change				
c. identify and monitor advocacy and change strategies that promote inclusion, equity, equality, and participatory democracy				
d. engage in community education efforts that promote social justice				

Field Placement Assignment

The majority of Social Service Worker programs require students to complete at least one if not a few pieces of academic work about their placement experience – this may be a case study, a process recording or an analysis of some aspect of their practice. Your Faculty Advisor will provide information on the expectations of any written work and the marking criteria that will be used to evaluate your submission. Assignments completed throughout the field placement should also be included in your professional development portfolio.

Final Review Meeting

The final review meeting is a chance to reflect on the placement and learning opportunities provided. Again, the agenda and meeting is typically led by the student. Evaluating the learning goals, objectives, and activities detailed in the learning contract and your perform-ance in relation to the program learning outcomes is the focal point of the final review meeting. The learning activities should be self-evaluated, as well as be evaluated by your Field Work Supervisor, the staff, and possibly your Faculty Advisor. This meeting provides an important opportunity to learn from the placement, improve it for future students and acknowledge the work of all involved.

Providing field placements can be immensely rewarding for an agency, organization or insti-tution and the individuals involved, but it is also a significant amount of work. Recognizing this and providing feedback helps ensure practicum sites feel valued and they are more likely to embark on the role again. Review Section F for guidance on how to effectively end a field placement.

Professional Development Portfolio

You should collect evidence of your skills and abilities to demonstrate that you have met the requirements for your program. Faculty Advisors may request a professional development portfolio at the end of your final field placement. A number of colleges are moving toward a professional development portfolio submission, which may contain key practice learning documents such as the learning contract, mid-term and final evaluations, evidence of your work, and reports. It is vital that you are clear from the beginning of the placement and know exactly what you are expected to submit at the end of the placement. Do not leave it to till the last minute! Remember also that whatever you are expected to submit, you must protect the confidentiality of clients. If you leave the names or any identifying features of your clients, you will fail your placement.

SUMMARY

There is a clear process to field placement learning. While this may be slightly different for students in different program or students placed in different agencies, organizations or institu-tions, it is useful for you to have a clear understanding of the general field placement process.

Roles and Responsibilities

3

There are typically three key players in setting up a field placement – you, the Field Work Supervisor, and the Faculty Advisor. In addition, the staff and management at the actual practicum site will also have key roles in making the experience successful and enjoyable for you.

Increasingly students are placed in field placement environments where there is no Field Work Supervisor on site. In this situation, a student will work with an onsite supervisor, who assigns tasks, and an offsite Field Work Supervisor who will work with the student and supervisor. In this situation, the onsite supervisor has a particularly important role. Offsite arrangements are discussed in more detail in Chapter 4.

In this section, the role and responsibilities of you as the student, the practicum site, the Field Work Supervisor, and Faculty Advisor are covered. It is important to remember that different programs may have specific requirements in terms of these roles. However, what follows is a general outline of the usual expectations in terms of roles and responsibilities.

Your Role as a Student

You will need to take responsibility for your own learning. It is important that you are proactive from the beginning of your placement.

Therefore you will need to:

- Submit the required documentation. Many programs required a completed Placement Agreement; this confirms the intent of the agency, organization or institution and the Field Work Supervisor to provide a field placement opportunity for you. The placement agreement outlines the days, hours, and time span that the student and field supervisor have negotiated and briefly identifies the nature of some of the experiences you will have at the agency, organization or institution.

- Attend all relevant placement meetings.

- Adhere to agency policies, procedures, and guidelines including the professional Code of Ethics and Standards of Practice.

- Recognize that you are to consider yourself a student within the agency, organization or institution and not a replacement for a paid worker, volunteer or apprentice. You are subject to the rules, regulations, and standards of professional conduct placed on other workers within that setting. In the event that a student contravenes the ethics and/or policies and procedures of the agency, organization or institution, the field placement could be terminated.

- Work in partnership with your Field Work Supervisor to devise a learning contract. You are required to complete a learning contract with the assistance of the Field Work Supervisor; this typically would take place after you have been oriented to the practicum site. The purpose of the learning contract is to ensure that both you and your Field Work Supervisor have clear and mutually agreed-upon learning goals, objectives and methods by which these objectives will be evaluated. It is the responsibility of students to submit the finalized learning contract to their Faculty Advisor. All three parties typically sign this contract.

- Be open and honest about your learning goals and objectives and highlight these at the learning contract meeting.

- Take responsibility for your actions throughout the placement and engage in all learning opportunities or activities provided.

- Carry an assigned workload while being increasingly self-directed.

- Perform work as required by your Field Work Supervisor in accordance with the agency, organization or institutional policy and practices.

- Account for your work in the same manner as other workers.

- Actively participate in the field placement process; this includes preparing for and participating in the Field Integration Seminars. Participation involves bringing service related material for discussion, identifying concerns about instruction and the agency, organization or institution, receiving and providing feedback and discussing other matters related to your learning.

- Attend regularly and be punctual. In the event of illness or personal emergency, you are expected to notify your field supervisor and faculty supervisor as soon as possible. This should be communicated before the start of your shift and most programs required students to make up missed hours.

- Interact professionally with staff at the agency, organization or institution.

- Be prepared to challenge your own thinking and that of others where appropriate and safe to do so.

- Use supervision effectively; attend regularly scheduled supervision meetings and taking initiative in preparing the agenda.

- Prepare any documentation (e.g., process records, reports, and audio-visual tapes) that is requested by the Field Work Supervisor for discussion at supervision meetings and to be receptive to the feedback provided.

- Provide evidence of your work in accordance with the program learning outcomes; submit Field Placements Activity Logs that accurately document placement hours and provide a brief description of daily activity.

- Actively participate in Field Integrative Seminars. Seminars provide an opportunity for you to discuss common concerns, gain practical insights and to practice effective problem solving, resource sharing and group membership and facilitation skills. You may be required to complete assignments related to your placement.

- Work in partnership with your Field Work Supervisor to complete the mid-term and final placement evaluations (or your program's equivalent). You are responsible for submitting evaluations to your Faculty Advisor by the dates required.

- Consolidate your learning through putting together a professional development portfolio detailing how you were able to achieve the program learning outcomes.

Practicum Site

The following guidelines are used to approve practicum sites for field placements:

- The practicum site has a philosophy of service that is compatible with the values and ethics of the social service worker profession, the developmental service worker or the child and youth worker profession.

- The practicum site must have policies regarding discrimination and harassment on the basis of age, economic status, gender, nationality, physical ability, political affiliation, race, religion or sexual preference.

- The practicum site offers students a range of learning opportunities and that these activities correspond with how the objectives for field placement will be evaluated.

- The practicum site needs to make available suitable space and working facilities for students, for instance, the use of a desk, privacy for interviewing, access to phones and equipment, office supplies, and transportation costs for out-of-office interviews and meetings.

- The practicum site shall ensure that a qualified staff member serve as Field Work Supervisor. For example a SSW student would normally have a field supervisor, who would have a SSW, BSW, MSW or equivalent with a minimum of two years post diploma/degree practice experience and be a member or eligible to be a member of OCSWSSW. In settings where an experienced staff member is willing to act as a supervisor, but does not possess a Social Service Worker diploma, the student is usually co-supervised by a staff member who holds a SSW, BSW, MSW or equivalent. A similar criteria is typically applied to Field Work Supervisors in the DSW and CYW field.

Staff

It is important for the staff of your agency, organization or institution to be able to effectively set up a field placement as they will impact your experience and what you will learn while on placement. The staff need to be "on board" and supportive of you coming to the practicum site.

Staff or an agency, organization or institution should:

- Be interested in participating in social service work, developmental service work or child and youth worker education.
- Be welcoming to you and support you to integrate into the team.
- Be willing to provide learning opportunities for you – such as allowing you to shadow their practice.
- Be willing to provide feedback about their views on your skills and abilities to you and to your Field Work Supervisor.
- Highlight any concerns as early as possible.

The management should:

- Ensure that staff members take responsibility for their role in the placement.
- Ensure that any work which is assigned to you is appropriate to your scope of practice and status as a student.
- Support the time and work allocated to the Field Work Supervisors to provide a student field placement; sufficient time needs to be allocated for student assignments, student orientation, preparation for and at least weekly supervision with the student, meetings with the Faculty Advisor, and the completion of field placement evaluations.

The role that staff and managers play in your field placement is critical to the success of the placement and the experiences which you and your Field Work Supervisor will have. If the staff and management are not fully committed and supportive of your being at the practicum site, this could impact your experience.

Field Work Supervisor

They are responsible for the overall management of the field placement and have essentially three roles:

Supervisory	Teaching	Assessment
• Prepare staff for a student field placement. • Liaison with other agencies, other professionals and colleagues to ensure opportunities and support are available to you.	• Supporting the development of an effective learning contract that specifies learning objectives, learning activities/opportunities and evaluation criteria with the student.	• Supporting you in being able to demonstrate that you have met the requirements for your program. • Create assessments that will give you evidence of of your work.

continued...

• Integrate your work with that of other staff. • Ensure that you have access to and adhere to relevant policies and procedures. • Take responsibility for the co-ordination of events in the case where concerns arise. • Attend all relevant meetings relating to the placement – usually a pre-placement meeting, learning contract meeting, mid-term and final review meeting. • Ensure accountability arrangements are clear and that effective support is in place. • Ensure that you have access to essential equipment (e.g., telephone and computer access) and that you have a place to sit and work.	• Orienting you to the community and the agency, organization or institution; arranging an appropriate orientation package and/or orientation program. • Selecting and making available to you appropriate learning opportunities. • Providing structured supervision sessions for you on a regular basis – generally weekly for a minimum of 60 to 90 minutes. • Providing you with the necessary informal supervision, advice, and guidance. • Supporting you in the development of an anti-oppressive framework to guide your practice skills. • Supporting you by linking theory to practice. For example, linking law and practice and values and practice.	• Assess your practice through direct observation. • Provide feedback to you about your skills and abilities including goals and objectives established in the learning contract. • Liaison with other relevant people to gather feedback about your practice. • Provide continuous feedback on your performance. • Writing reports about your progress on placement, which usually means a mid-term and final evaluation. • Making a recommendation about whether you have passed or failed the field placement. • Initiate procedures if you are failing or are marginally passing your field placement.

When the Field Work Supervisor is offsite, these responsibilities will be shared with the onsite supervisor (see Chapter 4).

Faculty Advisor

The responsibility of the Faculty Advisor lies predominantly within the academic setting.

The Faculty Advisor should:

- Initiate contact with the Field Work Supervisor by telephone at the beginning of the placement in order to make sure that the Field Work Supervisor has received and understood all the required forms and their submission deadlines: Placement Agreement, Mid-term Evaluations, Field Placement Activity Log, Learning Contract and Final Evaluation.

- Verify start date, days and hours of placement, expected completion date and placement supervision schedule for the student.

- Contribute at the pivotal points of the placement, for instance, learning contract, field integration seminars, mid-term and final evaluations meeting by arranging meetings with Field Work Supervisors and students.

- Facilitate the Field Integrative Seminar and provide you with instruction on field placement issues and concerns.

- Visit the agency, organization or institution as required ensuring that you are aware of the expectations of placements and to evaluate your progress.

- Orient new Field Work Supervisors with the program learning outcomes and expectation of field placement.

- Support you and your Field Work Supervisors to solve issues or conflicts regarding teaching, learning, and expectations.

- Terminate the field placement if the field placement is not satisfactory or if your performance in unsatisfactory.

- Evaluate your performance on field placement through consultation with you and your Field Work Supervisor.

- Evaluate your performance through reviewing the learning contract, the mid-term and final evaluations, the field integration assignments, and the field placement activity logs.

SUMMARY

There are a number of people involved in the provision of a field placement and each of them has a distinct role to play. You have the most important role to play. The rest of this guide will assist you in understanding your role and how to fulfill your responsibilities.

OFFSITE AND DISTANT FIELD PLACEMENTS ARRANGEMENTS

Offsite Field Placement Arrangements

Some agencies, organizations or institutions are willing and able to provide field placement learning opportunities for Social Service Worker students, but might not have anyone onsite who can act as a Field Work Supervisor. This is becoming more common with the increasing diversity in field placement environments and the increasingly rigorous requirements about who can act as a Field Work Supervisor. In these situations, a supervisor will be nominated from within the agency, organization or institution and a Field Work Supervisor who is based somewhere else will work with you. The Field Work Supervisor is then termed an offsite Field Work Supervisor, while the supervisor onsite may be referred to as an onsite supervisor, work based supervisor or job supervisor.

Offsite arrangements are sometimes referred to as tandem arrangements. This explains the system well – the Field Work Supervisor and onsite supervisor work in tandem to provide you with quality field placement learning opportunities.

There are various advantages to offsite field placement arrangements:

- You have two people providing you with support. This gives you access to a broader range of experiences.

- As the Field Work Supervisor works offsite, they will not be involved in office or agency politics and can provide an objective "sounding board" for you to discuss your experiences of working as part of the agency, organization or institution.

- The offsite Field Work Supervisor's time for supervision should be negotiated up front, so that you can be sure you receive the time you need.

However, these advantages will only be maximized if the arrangements are clear and the field placement is well organized. The key to this is ensuring there is a firm and clear agreement on how these roles will work for you. It is the Field Work Supervisor's responsibility to negotiate this, but you need to be proactive in making sure that you know how the arrangement will work best for you.

It is helpful to view the key relationships in offsite arrangements using a triangulation model as follows. The triangulation model emphasizes the importance of the three key players in the placement to have a close working relationship to the other two (see Figure 1). Sometimes, the relationships may not always be so well defined or developed. In some situations the triangle looks more like Figure 2. Using this visual image, it is clear that where relationships are not clearly defined, then the support in the placement is not as secure and consequently, impacts the quality of your experience.

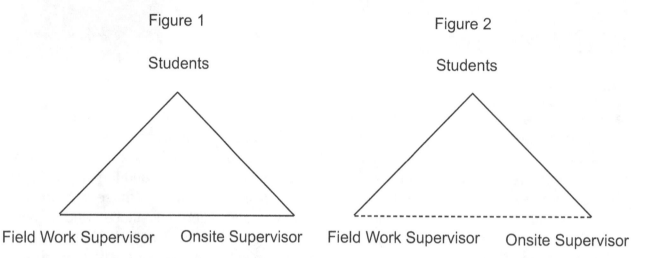

Figure 1

Students

Field Work Supervisor   Onsite Supervisor

Figure 2

Students

Field Work Supervisor   Onsite Supervisor

It is important to negotiate the terms of your relationships at the beginning of field placement. The Faculty Advisor, the OnSite Supervisor and the Field Work Supervisor work in cooperation with one another as indicated in the following diagram:

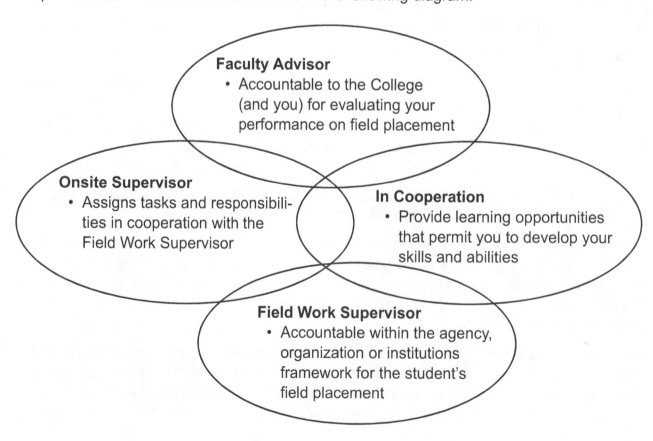

Faculty Advisor
• Accountable to the College (and you) for evaluating your performance on field placement

Onsite Supervisor
• Assigns tasks and responsibilities in cooperation with the Field Work Supervisor

In Cooperation
• Provide learning opportunities that permit you to develop your skills and abilities

Field Work Supervisor
• Accountable within the agency, organization or institutions framework for the student's field placement

The best starting point for negotiating arrangements is to think together with your Onsite Supervisor and Field Work Supervisor about all of the key tasks that need to be undertaken during the placement and then negotiate the division of these tasks.

In every offsite situation, the way in which the relationships work and the way that the tasks are divided will be different. The key to a successful placement is clear negotiation prior to the start of the placement about who will do what, when, and how. This should be regularly reviewed during the placement and should be open to change as necessary.

The framework on the following page can help you to consider who might do what in a placement where your Field Work Supervisor is offsite. Remember you can adapt the table, for instance, arrange taks in terms of priority. Where you are working with a Field Work Supervisor onsite, you may still find it useful to work through the table to clarify what you will do and what your Field Work Supervisor will do.

Exactly who does what will depend on a number of factors including the nature of the field placement, the experiences of all involved, and the work load of those involved.

Setting up the supervision is a key issue. This may be difficult to arrange. The Onsite Supervisor will always be the one to provide the day-to-day informal supervision that you will need – they will be there in the agency, organization or institution when you have immediate questions. Regular, formal supervision must be provided by the Field Work Supervisor – as this is a key element for being able to provide feedback and evaluate performance. However, outside of these basics, supervision responsibilities can become blurred. Since the Onsite Supervisor is accountable for the work which you carry out, she or he will also need to carry out some formal supervision in line with placement requirements. The danger is that if supervision responsibilities are not clearly negotiated, you may feel "over supervised." You may feel like you are repeating yourself and covering the same issues in two separate supervision sessions. To address this, some practicum sites will arrange occasional joint supervision or co-supervision sessions where both Field Supervisors and Onsite Supervisors attend. It is not uncommon for these meetings to be held through a tele-conference, especially if it is a distant field placement. These sessions generally only include both Onsite Supervisor and Field Work Supervisor for half of the session and then you and the Field Work Supervisor have half the session alone. This can work really well in some situations, but it is important to agree carefully how you want this to work and periodically review how effective this is for you. Remember, it is your field placement and you need these arrangements to work for you!

SUMMARY

Essentially, the role of the Field Work Supervisor is divided between two people in offsite placement arrangements. However, the Offsite Field Work Supervisor retains overall responsibility for supervising the field placement. The key to making sure off site field placement arrangements work is have clear communication and clarity about roles and responsibilities.

Negotiating Responsibilities				
Task	**To be carried out by**			**Notes**
	Student	Field Work Supervisor	Onsite Supervisor	
Field placement request				
Preparing staff for student field placement				
Setting up field placement resources (i.e., desk)				
Field placement interview				
Writing learning contract				
Preparing orientation material				
Devising student orientation				
Devising learning opportunities and activities				
Supervision: Formal				
Work load assignment				
Direct observation of your field placement activities				
Obtaining feedback from clients				
Obtaining feedback from staff				
Mid-term evaluation				
Mid-term review meeting				
Documenting evidence of work				
Contributing to final placement evaluation				
Final evaluation				
Final review meeting				
Professional Development Portfolio				

EXAMINING THE IMPACT OF POWER WITHIN THE FIELD PLACEMENT PROCESS

5

Field placements provide a valuable learning experience, yet the process itself creates an unequal role relationship. Both the Field Work Supervisor and the Faculty Advisor occupy an authority role which is intrinsically more powerful than yours. People being evaluated may feel resistant to the evaluation process. They may also fear or feel anxious towards the Field Work Supervisor or Faculty Advisor due to this power imbalance. Past experiences influence expectations and students who bring with them painful or unjust experiences of learning and assessment may find the prospect of field placement particularly intimidating. Students with visible or invisible differences which could make them the target of discrimination may have specific concerns about being treated fairly.

In order to work effectively with the power differentials inherent in the field placement process, it is important to have a clear understanding of the different forms of power which may operate within the relationship you have with your Field Work Supervisor and your Faculty Advisor.

Professional / Expert Power

As a learner you are referred to as a student, your Field Work Supervisor is a worker (often a very experienced and additionally qualified worker) and will be seen as the expert. The professional opinion of Field Work Supervisor is likely to be given more weight than yours, for example, and this can lead to you feeling powerless, especially if there are differences of opinion around your performance. Students with previous working experience may be more aware of this power differential. You may have previously held professional power and now feel that you have lost this. This may make you feel particularly de-skilled. This would be a valuable discussion to have with your field work Supervisor.

The way people perceive professional power is revealed by responses such as "I don't want to speak to a student...I want to speak to a real social worker." Other common comments include "well, he's only a student..." or "she's just a student." Most students have experienced comments that devalue their role as students. Field Work Supervisor can offer you support and advice on how best to deal with this. This topic will likely be discussed during Field Integration Seminars, both your Faculty Advisor and peers may also provide support on how to deal with this.

Resource Power

Field Work Supervisor and Faculty Advisor are likely to have more knowledge than you about local community resources. including field placement resources. This knowledge can be used to support you to access opportunities and minimize the resource power imbalance.

Societal Power

Societal power is basically power derived from the oppression of certain groups in society. Field Work Supervisor and Faculty Advisor hold societal power in terms of the way society differentiates between the status of a "teacher" and a "student."

> Through socialization and society we view people based on many things we have learned to be "right." In an anti-oppressive framework, these views are broken into six main lenses; racism, sexism, heterosexism, ableism, ageism, and class oppression. Many of the biases we have as workers enter our practice without us being aware of them. (Moore, 2001)

Societal power dynamics based on forms of oppression such as racism, sexism and ableism can go either way – so that students may hold some societal power. For example, where a black woman Field Work Supervisor is working with a white male student, the student will hold societal power both in terms of race and gender.

Field Work Supervisors exercise some form of authority over students, and this imbalance of power can lead to exploitation if people are not aware. Your Field Work Supervisor and Faculty Advisor will likely discuss this form of power with you in terms of differences which exist between you as it can assist you in your understanding of oppression within society and within individual relationships.

The Power to Determine

This form of power may be at the forefront on your mind when you begin field placement. The power to determine is what separates the power held by Field Work Supervisor and Faculty Advisor. Faculty Advisor are responsible for making recommendation about whether you have passed or failed a placement and so "determine" your future. While feedback from a Field Work Supervisor and others is important and will be used to inform the Faculty Advisor's decision, your final grade is determined by the Faculty Advisor. The power to determine will impact the relationship between you and your Faculty Advisor. Your Faculty Advisor will likely discuss this power differential and negotiate how you will manage the impact of these together.

Addressing the Power Imbalance

It is tempting to ignore power differentials and therefore not discuss them. You may feel anxious about having these power differentials highlighted; however, everyone involved in your placement already is aware of the power dynamics and it is important to be open about how imbalances of power will be dealt with.

The same kinds of power differentials exist in every professional relationship, for example, between workers and clients, and between different professionals. Discussing this with your Field Work Supervisor and considering the similarities in your own relationships with clients can be a useful exercise. For example, if you consider the relationships between you and clients, we can see how these power differentials apply:

- Professional / expert power – the clients will see you as a professional with expertise
- Resource power – you are likely to have more knowledge about the resources available to clients than they do
- Societal power – the same differences will exist between you and clients. You will hold some societal power by the very fact that the client is a client and the stigma associated with this status
- The power to determine – you may be carrying out an assessment of the client and therefore have the power to determine. For example, you may be making a recommendation about whether a client meets eligibility criteria

Discussing the power dynamics inherent in all professional relationships in this way and considering where you feel the power lies can be a good learning experience. Through having these discussions, you begin to appreciate the "safety nets" which are in place to ensure that power is not abused. For example, everyone involved in field placement is working to policies and procedures, codes of ethics and standards of practice, and formal complaints procedures exist – all of this can provide a safety net to ensure that the Field Work Supervisor and Faculty Advisor and you all use the power you have responsibly.

Other important aspects to ensuring that you do not feel powerless include:

Learning Empowerment

You will be familiar with the principles of empowerment. To be empowered, people need to know as much as possible about what is going to happen and why. You and your Field Work Supervisor can work together to ensure you feel empowered by:

- Being clear about the field placement process and how your performance will be assessed
- Creating an enabling environment where your questions are encouraged
- Creating learning activities and opportunities that are within your scope of practice
- Promoting partnership
- Providing accessible and relevant written and verbal information

Complaints and Appeals Procedures

All colleges will have a clearly written complaints and appeals procedure. You need to be well informed about appeals and complaints procedures and you need to feel confident about using when necessary.

You should raise any concerns that you have with your Faculty Advisor and Field Work Supervisor. Raising concerns will not be held against you. Students are generally very reluctant to raise any concerns because they are so aware of the power differentials. It is important that you feel as comfortable and as safe as possible to raise any concerns.

TOP TIPS FOR ADDRESSING POWER ISSUES IN FIELD PLACEMENT

- Discuss power differentials rather than denying them
- Look for ways to be empowered
- Be clear about the field placement process and how you will be assessed
- Work in partnership with your Faculty Advisor and Field Work Supervisor
- Ask questions
- Be familiar with complaints and concerns procedures

SUMMARY

The power differentials in field placement are undeniable. It is essential that these are acknowledged and discussed together with your Field Work Supervisor and Faculty Advisor. Understanding the power differential that you face puts you more in tuned with the power differentials that your clients may face.

MANAGING EXPECTATIONS

6

To conclude this section on the field placement process, roles and responsibilities, we summarize key expectations.

What your placement will expect of you	What you can expect from your placement	What to do if you don't get what you expect
Commitment – this implies attending, being punctual, and following through with workload assignments.	You can expect everyone involved in organizing the placement to be committed to providing you with a quality learning experience.	Talk to your Field Work Supervisor and Faculty Advisor if you feel you are not getting the range of learning activities and opportunities you need to meet your goals and objectives. Ask for a meeting with your Field Work Supervisor and other staff involved with your field placement. Ask for a meeting with your Field Work Supervisor and Faculty Advisor if you remain dissatisfied.
Professionalism – the staff, the management and your Field Work Supervisor will expect you to conform to the OCSWSSW Code of Ethics and Standards of Practice and adhere to the values that guide your profession.	You should expect staff to act professionally and follow the same OCSWSSW Code of Ethics and Standards of Practice. You should expect your Faculty Advisor and Field Work Supervisor to promote anti-oppressive practice and to assess and evaluate your performance in a fair and transparent way.	If you are concerned about the conduct of others, check the agency, organizational or institutional policies and procedures provided during your orientation. Remember, each agency, organization or institution will have an organizational structure with clear reporting procedures. You are to raise concerns with individuals

continued...

If concerns are raised about your skills and abilities during the placement, you are expected to act on these quickly. The Field Work Supervisor and staff will not want you to fail, but they will want to maintain the best possible service for clients.

You should be able to discuss and act on constructive feedback which others give you in order to assist you in learning and developing.

You should expect to receive feedback throughout the placement. There should be no surprises in your mid-term or final evaluations. You should also expect to provide feedback on the quality of the field placement experience.

first, and take matters higher as appropriate.

If you have concerns around your assessments or feedback, this should be discussed with your Field Work Supervisor first. Your Faculty Advisor could be a valuable source of support and a three-way meeting may be necessary to move matters forward.

Take initiative by asking for feedback on your performance.

If feedback is not forthcoming, talk to your Field Work Supervisor. Again, involve your Faculty Advisor if necessary.

Accountability – Linked with professional conduct above, a certain amount of trust will be placed in you during your placement. This may be trust around finances, case management, representing the services provided to other agencies, or around being professional. Your Field Work Supervisor will also expect you to demonstrate good judgment by being able to explain and justify your actions with clients. Exercising solid judgement is part of how your performance will be evaluated.

In return, you should also expect your Field Work Supervisor and Faculty Advisor be accountable for their actions and decisions. In addition, towards the end of your placement(s), you are likely to be able to expect a greater degree of independence and autonomy around your workload. However, the person who is responsible for your work on site will remain involved and have overall responsibility for the safety of your field placement.

Being open about your work will enable others to build trust in you. If there are issues with trust, an open dialogue is the first means of enabling better communication-tackling issues as soon as they arise can also enable you to demonstrate that you are competent and have good judgement.

continued...

You will be expected to make effective use of supervision. Your placement will expect you to identify any areas where you need support and to take action in these areas.	You can expect to be supported. (i.e., Referrals to counselling department, help lines, support groups or Field Integration Seminars) The Field Work Supervisor, the staff and your Faculty Advisor are not there to support or "social work" you with personal crises or issues. It is important that you seek this support outside of the placement setting and in particular, do not draw staff into such issues as it can reflect badly on you. It is critical that personal and professional boundaries are in place.	Find out what community supports employees use and whether you are able to access these at the start of your placement. Seek any support or professional development within the placement setting and from sources outside the placement environment Keep Field Work Supervisor and staff informed around any personal issues which may affect your work, just as you would as an employee. However, if issues become unmanageable, then do not be afraid to ask for time off as sometimes "carrying on regardless" can be too much of a struggle in a situation which is already stressful for you.

SUMMARY

An important part of setting up a successful field placement experience, it to manage the expectation of all parties involved with the placement. Make sure you are clear about the expectations at the onset of the placement. Field placement is a two-way process – you can expect to get out of it what you put into it. You can expect certain things from your placement, but don't forget that you have probably the most important role to play.

KEY LEARNING POINTS: SECTION A

- Field placement is a significant part of your training requirements

- There is a clear process to field placement. Having a clear understanding of this will help to ease anxiety about your placement

- Everyone involved in field placement has an important role to play. Understanding everyone's role and responsibilities will help to improve your placement experience

- If you have a placement with offsite Field Work Supervisors, you need to understand the difference between the roles of your On Site Supervisor and offsite Field Work Supervisor

- Power dynamics can have a significant impact on field placement. Clarity around this will assist in ensuring you have a positive placement experience

- You need to be proactive and take initiative in all aspects of field placement – you must not see yourself as a passive recipient of learning

- You get out of field placement what you put into it!

GETTING A PLACEMENT

B

Most programs of study do not allow students to "find" their own placement, so to some extent the title of this section might seem misleading. However, this section will help you to consider how you are matched with a placement and how you can influence this effectively. It will also explore the advantages and disadvantages of different types of placements. Finally, this section concludes with a chapter exploring what Field Work Supervisors are looking for in students, as understanding this can significantly help you in "getting a placement."

HOW DO I GET A PLACEMENT?

On the positive side you don't need to go and knock on doors or spend days "cold calling" potential placement providers. In fact, most Colleges do not allow students to make their own arrangements for placements, even if they want to.

While there is the exception, students are generally required to participate in a field placement outside of their regular workplace. However, the vast majority of students are placed in an agency, organization or institution with which they have no prior links.

Colleges are responsible for providing you with field placement opportunities and many colleges have a Field Coordinator with a Field Liaison (or a Field Preparation Faculty) who has the responsibility for matching students to field placement opportunities. They will look for appropriate placements for all students. However, as you will know, some regions may have a shortage of field placements and they will not be able to place everyone in their "first choice" setting. You should be prepared to travel quite some distance to your placement and should be open to experiencing placements in a wide range of settings.

Depending on the area in which you are studying, you might find that there are certain things that can make you "difficult to place." For example, if you don't have access to your own transport, the Field Coordinator is likely to have much more limited options as many agencies, organizations or institutions need students who have their own transportation. It can feel very demoralizing if you are one of the last students in your class or among your peers to be placed. Everyone will be talking about their placement and you still don't know where you are going. You can learn a lot from this about how clients may feel at times – it certainly helps you to empathize with children and young people who are labelled as "difficult to place."

You can help the field placement matching process in a number of ways by:

- not panicking! You will get a placement. The worst case scenario is you might start a little later than your peers, but you can use the time to make sure you are fully prepared
- making sure your field placement request form is well completed and doesn't close off too many options (see chapter 8)
- ensuring that your cover letter/resume is up to date and reflects all that you have to offer a practicum setting

- organizing your professional development portfolio to highlight what you have accomplished both academically as well as through your community involvement

- getting to know your Field Coordinator and or Field Preparation Faculty. Keep in regular contact with them and respond to any communication from them in a timely manner

- approaching the process as an opportunity for learning

- being open to whatever opportunities are offered to you – you may have to accept a placement some distance from your home.

- talking to your Field Coordinator and or Field Preparation Faculty about any opportunities you might be aware of that they may not already use is beneficial. While they will not allow you to make arrangements for your own placement, they might be able to build on any links or ideas you have to arrange a placement for you, especially for students who may be wanting to return home for their field placement. Some students, for example, return to their hometown for field placements – others may be going to live some distance away from the College. Field Coordinator and or Field Preparation Faculty can sometimes arrange placements in areas some distance away with some advice and assistance from you.

SUMMARY

Placements can be in short supply depending on the region. You need to make sure you are aware of how the process of placement matching works in your College, so that you can take a proactive part in getting a placement. Don't be tempted to "break the rules" and don't be closed off to new ideas or suggestions.

THE FIELD PLACEMENT REQUEST FORM

8

Whatever process your College uses to match students to placements, you are likely to be asked to complete a field placement request form or a personal profile. Most Colleges provide a questionnaire for you to complete prior to being matched with a placement.

In many cases hundreds of field placement request forms are submitted to Field Work Supervisors and unfortunately many of them are very poorly completed. One can only surmise that students who have completed these did not understand the importance of these forms – perhaps they rushed through them, thinking that no one but their Faculty Advisor or Field Preparation Faculty (who knows them anyway) would see them.

However, the importance of these documents cannot be under-estimated. They will no doubt be used in different ways and be seen by different people. A brief explanation of the process used by most colleges in Ontario is provided

> Student completes a field placement request form (sample provided at the end of the chapter)

> Student submits a field placement request form, cover letter, resume, and professional development portfolio to field preparation faculty

> Field prepartion faculty may add some additional comments to the field placement request form. Eligibility for field placement is confirmed and then request form is passed on to the field corrdinator within the college

> Field liason will schedule a meeting with the student and field coordinator for the purpose of placement matching

> After the field coordinator matches you to a practicum site, student will be instructed on how to go about initiating the field placement interview with field work supervisor

continued...

Field work supervisor schedules interview with you and in some cases there may be several students who may interview for a particular practicum site

↓

Field work supervisor decides whether to offer a field placement to you

Understanding this process should help you to see that potentially a large number of people may see your request form. They may screen you out of a potential placement based on what they see on the form. So you really need to put a great deal of thought and effort into what and how you present yourself on this form. If you use shorthand or don't structure a sentence well, it's likely that a potential Field Work Supervisor may think you won't be able to document work effectively, for example.

The Request for Placement form, the cover letter and resume are used to screen who will be contacted for an interview in some cases. Field Work Supervisors have expressed concern with the quality of some of the submissions. In fact, some Field Work Supervisors have indicated that these submissions were like someone had "scribbled a few words on the back of a napkin." Field Coordinators across the province will agree that the best quality placement requests are almost always the ones to be placed first. Most Field Work Supervisors are extremely busy, and don't want to spend time trying to figure whether or not the student is suitable for the practicum site.

> **TOP TIPS FOR MAKING PLACEMENT REQUESTS**
>
> - Don't rule out placements suggestions made by Faculty and Field Coordinators.
> - Create a professional Field Placement Request.
> - Put time into your cover letter, resume and professional development portfolio and make sure it shows.
> - Think about what a Field Work Supervisor will be looking for and reflect this in your submission.

Reverse the actual situation for a moment. Imagine there are only a few students and lots of placements "competing" to get you. You're sent lots of placement requests about placements and get to choose – will you go for the one with hardly any information on it, that's badly written or would you go for one that's well constructed and that someone has obviously spent time on?

- Seek advice on how best to complete your Field Placement Request form, your cover letter and your resume.
- Proof read what you produce – maybe even ask a friend to do so (you often miss your own mistakes).

- If your placement request is handwritten (it is usually best to produce it on the computer) then make sure your writing is legible.

- Never use "text speak"! (You'd be surprised how many people do.)

- Clearly and concisely identify your unique "selling" points – you might have very limited experience but you will have skills and abilities which make you an ideal candidate for field (after all that's how you got into the program!)

- If the form asks you for placement preferences, don't be too specialized or specific. Lots of people ask for placements in highly specialized areas (e.g., Children's Aid Society or Youth Offender Facilities). By the very nature of these being highly specialized, there are not many placements available in these areas and when Field Work Supervisors in other settings see this, they will think "this student does not want what we have to offer" and move on to another placement request. You might then end up one of the last students to be placed. If you really want a placement in child welfare write: "I'm interested in working with children and young people, particularly those with mental health issues." You could get a Children's Aid Society placement, but it will also open up a lot more opportunities for you which will give you similar experiences.

- Avoid vague statements about "being good with people" or "wanting to help people." Focus on *why* you are good and *how* you see your role in supporting people.

- Field Work Supervisors see lots of submissions – how can you ensure your submission stands out?

- Think about what Field Work Supervisor are looking for (see Chapter 10 for advice on this) and try to ensure that you capture this in your submission.

A sample of the Field Placement Request Form that was created for students applying for field placement is provided on the following page. This form could be used for all programs of study. It is important that students take the time to complete this form. In addition to this form, students need to ensure that their resume and cover letter are professional and tailored to the sector that they are interested in pursuing a field placement.

SAMPLE FIELD PLACEMENT REQUEST FORM

The purpose of the form is to compile pertinent information for planning and decision making regarding field placement. When completed, information in this form will be shared with potential field placement sites in preparation for the pre-placement interview. This form is to be submitted to the Field Coordinator with a cover letter and current resume.

☐ Field Practice I Fall Semester   Application Due:

☐ Field Practice I Winter Semester   Application Due:

☐ Field Practice I Summer Semester   Application Due:

1. IDENTITFYING INFORMATION:

Name: Student   Number:

Address:

City: Province: Postal Code:

Telephone: Telephone (Work/Cell):

Student email address:

Language Proficiency (other than English):

2. PRE-REQUISITES AND SUPPORTING DOCUMENTS:

Please indicate, by checking the corresponding box, whether you have met the following requirements:

☐ Eligibility for Field Placement Status Report

☐ Eligibility for criminal reference check

☐ Cover Letter and Resume has been sent electronically to the Field Coordinator

☐ Immunization Records

☐ Certification for NVCI

☐ Certification for ASST

☐ Certification for First Aid/CPR

☐ Profession Development Portfolio

3. GEOGRAPHIC LOCATION:

Please list your top three geographic locations for field placement in order of preference:

1)

2)

3)

4. POPULATION PREFERENCE:

- ☐ Children
- ☐ Adolescents
- ☐ Adults
- ☐ Elderly
- ☐ Women
- ☐ Men
- ☐ Families
- ☐ Groups
- ☐ Immigrants
- ☐ Aboriginal
- ☐ Communities
- ☐ Other:

5. PREFERRED PRIMARY CLASSIFICATION:

- ☐ Abuse
- ☐ Addictions
- ☐ Adoption
- ☐ Advocacy
- ☐ AIDS/HIV
- ☐ Alzheimer's Dementia
- ☐ Child Welfare
- ☐ Community Development
- ☐ Community Services
- ☐ Community Corrections
- ☐ Court/Justice
- ☐ Institution
- ☐ Crisis Intervention
- ☐ Day Treatment
- ☐ Death/Dying
- ☐ Developmental Disabilities
- ☐ Domestic Violence

- ☐ Early childhood Services
- ☐ Educational Support
- ☐ Elder Care
- ☐ End of Life Care
- ☐ Family Service
- ☐ Faith-based Organization
- ☐ Foster Care
- ☐ Forensic Psychiatry
- ☐ Gay/Lesbian/LGBT Issues
- ☐ Government
- ☐ Health Care Housing
- ☐ Homelessness
- ☐ Immigrant Settlement Services
- ☐ Legal Issues
- ☐ Long-term Care
- ☐ Oppression & Injustice
- ☐ Poverty

- ☐ Physical Disabilities
- ☐ Public Welfare
- ☐ Mental Health
- ☐ Multicultural
- ☐ Residential Correctional
- ☐ Residential Treatment
- ☐ Residential Disabilities
- ☐ Residential-Adult
- ☐ Residential-Child
- ☐ School Based Programs
- ☐ Sexual Abuse
- ☐ Social Policy
- ☐ Special Education
- ☐ Substance Abuse Prevention
- ☐ Vocational Services
- ☐ Volunteer-Based
- ☐ Youth Based Service

My top three primary classifications are:

1.

2.

3.

Note: All placements must be arranged in consultation with the Field Coordinator. Students must not initiate contact with any agency to seek a placement with that agency without prior approval. Any placement initiated without the knowledge of the Field Coordinator may not be approved.

6. OTHER CONSIDERATION FOR FIELD PLANNING:

a) Describe how your previous experience (employment, volunteer and/or co-op placement) contribute to this field placement request.

b) Discuss the strengths and skills which you bring to the field placement.

c) Describe what knowledge and skills you hope to acquire during the field placement.

d) Identify your short-term and long-term professional goals.

e) Do you have a vehicle for field placement?

f) Are you willing to update any immunizations that may be required to partake in field placement?

g) Do you agree to abide by the Social Service Code of Ethic in your field placement?

h) Are you aware that violations to the Code of Ethics can lead to termination of your field placement?

i) Do you agree to follow the Schools policies and procedure regarding field placement?

j) Do you have a particular field placement agency or primary classification (not listed) that you would like to explore? If so, please explain.

k) Will you require any accommodation for your field placement?

Please note that many practicum settings now require students to obtain a police records check and/or criminal records check. This can take 6-8 weeks. Students are encouraged to apply for this in advance of the commencement of the practicum.

RELEASE OF INFORMATION:

I hereby authorize the Field Coordinator to release information provided in the Field Placement Request Form, Resume and field placement application to potential field placement agencies and Field Work Supervisors.

☐ Yes, I consent
☐ No, I do not consent

Date: _____ Signature: _____

SUMMARY

Placement matching is generally a paper exercise – Field Placement Coordinators will try to match you with an appropriate placement based on your field placement request, your cover letter and resume, and in some cases your professional development portfolio. Never under-estimate the importance of these submissions to the screening process!

FIELD PLACEMENT IN THE PUBLIC AND PRIVATE SECTOR

9

There is always a demand by students to complete field placement within the public sector. This is a challenge given the current lack of placements in various levels of government. Despite the the few placement opportunities available in the public sector, many students still will request this type of placement. Some students believe that experience in the public sector will help them when they go to look for work. While the public sector tends to be unionized with starting salaries that may be higher than in other sectors, placement opportunities in the commercial and voluntary sector are equally rewarding.

Students are often placed in non-traditional settings when they really wanted to be in a traditional government placement. Many of these students change their views as the placement progresses. Field placements in non-traditional settings like the commercial and voluntary sector can be every bit as good as those in public sectors – and many are better! This chapter will help you to understand the different types of placements opportunities.

A field placement can be provided in any setting where community and/or human services might take place. The potential list is almost endless. Here are some examples:

Advocacy services
Addictions services
Business that provide care
Community-based health care
Community based social services
Community based mental health
Community centers
Court and justice service
Day treatment programs
Detox
Domestic violence
Education
Elderly care
Crisis centers
Faith based organizations
Family service
Health care

Homeless shelters
Multicultural centers
Long-term care facilities
Legal services – advocacy services
Outpatient mental health
Police, probation and correctional settings
Poverty
Prevention Services
Rehabilitation program
Residential treatment-Adult
Residential treatment-children
Respite care
Schools
Settlement service
Therapeutic recreational services
Volunteer-based programs
Youth Offenders

The purpose of a field placement is to provide students with practical, integrated learning experiences and a body of knowledge related to the promotion of human well-being and the affirmation of strengths and capacities of people in their environments.

Non-traditional placements may be able to offer you rich experiences in the field. Legal, social and political issues at the local, provincial and national levels set the parameters and organizations service delivery models. It is important to understand how human service organizations are classified in order to appreciate how to identify what setting you would like to do your field placement.

What is an Organization?

The practice of social work has traditionally been carried out in organizational settings; these organizational settings are classified based on auspices or operating authority. Holland (1995) defines organizations as "formalized groups of people who make coordinated use of resources and skills to accomplish given goals or purposes" (Holland, 1995).

Different Types of Organizations

Organizations are classified based on three factors: operating authority or legal basis, characteristic of the client group being served and or the services being provided (Gibelman & Furman, 2008). Operating authority refers to the parameters within which an organization can function; therefore, identifying what types of activities an organization can do and how they can go about doing it. For example, how an organization raises money, their governance structure, how they recruit and use volunteers and staff and provide service is determined primarily through operating authority.

Types and Characteristics of Service Organizations in Canada

Public Organizations

Public Sector

- Concerned with social welfare (which implies a collective and public responsibility for the well-being of society), programs and commonly referred to as municipal, provincial, and federal levels of government or divisions of government, are typically funded through tax dollars in full or in part.

- Purpose of the organization is linked to legal codes and government regulations (Horejsi & Garthwait, 2004).

- Governance is dictated by statute (legislation) or is an extension of a public organization with which a clear administrative relationship exists.

- Provide certain types of service that not-for-profit and private agencies may not provide, for example, primary services in which the organization acts as a representative or the government, such as in child or adult protective services.

Private Organizations

Voluntary Sector

- Not-for-profit or non-profit organizations originated in the historical philanthropy movement; the formation of voluntary organizations to solve community problems predates the industrial era.

- The origins of social work as a profession are rooted in providing non-profit charity organizations with services and are separate from the government.

- Volunteer-friendly (Saunders, 2004).

- Organized as corporations and legally bound to an internal organizational structure that is self-governing, such as a Board of Directors.

- Board of Directors represent the interests of the community or group that the organization seeks to serve and supports the organizations work.

- Revenues raised must be used to support organizations programs and services; held publically accountable for their activities.

- Empowered to hire employees to carry out the mission of the organization and solicit charitable contributions to support their organization (Holland, 1995; Horejsi & Garthwait, 2004).

Commercial Sector

- Privately owned and operated organizations that employ human service workers including SSW, CYW, and DSW; their purpose is to provide direct practical care.

- Relatively new, the commercial sector, also known as proprietary organizations include long-term care facilities, residential treatment facilities, health care and child day care centers.

- Changes in federal funding regulations have been linked to the creation of the commercial sector; therefore, permitting commercial organizations to apply for and compete for contract funds (Gibelman, 1998).

- Cannot solicit charitable contributions; private business that yield profits.

Most community organizations establish clear identities through having mission statements. The purpose of an organization may be predetermined through legislative or funding mandates or may be determined more locally by staff, administrators and/or Board of Governors, all of which are known as operating authority or auspice. The mission statement of an agency, organization or institution sets out the rationale for its existence, including the client group it intends to serve and the community needs or problems that it seeks to address.

Placements in the Commercial Sector

Students offered placements in the commercial sector are typically involved in providing direct practical care. Often such field placements are in residential treatment setting with opportunities for direct clinical practice. It is useful to consider some of the advantages as well as disadvantages of commercial sector placements, so that you can go into such a placement setting prepared and informed.

Advantages of Commercial Sector Placements

- *Values*: Commercial sector placements can enable you to consolidate some of your learning around the skills and values of the profession. The focus of social service work is around the empowerment of vulnerable people; a commercial sector placement can really help you to appreciate some of the key challenges involved in making empowerment real for those who require a substantial amount of support.

- *Communication*: Being part of a service which provides people with direct care and support can develop your basic communication skills and documentation skills.

- *Creativity*: A commercial sector placement can mean that you have the opportunity to think "outside the box" and develop your skills of creativity. Public sector field placements can be restrictive because of the very nature of statutory duties, and direct care placements can enable you to work more creatively and apply your theoretical knowledge around person-centred planning into practice. It may be much easier to plan and deliver group work in a commercial sector setting than in public sector field placement.

- *Interprofessional Team*: As social service workers increasingly work as part of a interprofessional team, providing direct care can be helpful in developing your knowledge of the roles and responsibilities of professionals with nursing, therapeutic or other backgrounds. Direct service provision is often delivered in a multi-agency context therefore enabling you to meet goals around engaging with a wide range of other professionals.

- *Developing the team*: Being placed in a position where you provide direct care can also help the team to develop their knowledge and understanding of social service workers' roles and functions.

- *Benefits for Clients*: Your placement may mean that clients actually get more specialized input into their person-directed care plans and you may be able to make valuable suggestions and contributions to their care.

- *Autonomy*: Sometimes, being placed in a direct care setting can mean that you learn the skills of working independently and in a self-directed way.

- *Developing an understanding of leadership and management*: Students providing direct care often work alongside managers and may be given opportunities to attend management meetings in a way that students in public sector settings do not. This can provide students with unique insights into leadership and into the workings of organizations.

Possible Disadvantages and What to Do?

- *Being viewed "an extra pair of hands."* While there is value in you being involved in providing some aspects of direct service care, you have to meet the requirements of your field placement and it is important that you are not seen as another member of the staff. The negotiations around your responsibilities in your learning contract is essential to making your placement work for you and ensuring everyone is clear around the purpose of your placement and the requirements you need to fulfill.

- *Lack of clarity about your goals for field placement*: Linked with the issues discussed above, placements in direct care settings work best when the staff are clear as to how you will be evaluated, their role in providing you with opportunities to demonstrate that you have met the program outcomes. Some discussion with the staff around the roles and responsibilities is helpful and your Field Work Supervisor should ensure that everyone has this clarity. The role of the on-site supervisor (or your Field Work Supervisor if they are on-site with you) is vital to ensuring that everybody has a clear and shared understanding of your role and its boundaries.

- *Gathering Evidence For Your Portfolio*: You need to be offered a good range of learning activities which will support you in meeting your learning goals and objectives, as well as the opportunity to gather the evidence for your professional development portfolio. Again, this is why negotiating your learning needs and the learning contract are key to successful placements in the commercial sector. Delivering hands on care is important, but you also need to develop skills in assessment, planning, advocacy, group work and all of the other areas which your peers in field work placements will be working on.

- *Feeling isolated*: In settings where there is no other social service workers employed, you may feel isolated. This is where the support of your Field Work Supervisor, Faculty Advisor, peers and others may need to come into play. Networking and developing your professional links also helps you to meet your learning goals.

Placements in the Voluntary Sector

Large voluntary organizations increasingly deliver a range of functions on behalf of local authorities, and small charitable organizations or community groups can also offer rich learning experiences.

Advantages of Voluntary Sector Placements

- *Creativity*: The range of opportunities within the voluntary sector is vast. For example, large children's organizations run services around caring for young children, family support, family mediation, leaving care, children's centres, and lots more. A placement with one service may open up opportunities for links with others. These placements may also enable you to be creative in your practice and to try new ways of working.

- *Promoting Innovation*: Voluntary sector placements offer opportunity to promote innovation in areas such as community development. With fewer limitations, students and qualified workers are permitted to try new approaches.

- *Developing interprofessional learning*: Some organizations have a range of employees from different professional backgrounds.

- **Opening up your career options**: The voluntary sector can open your eyes to new fields and specialized areas which you may really enjoy working in.

- *Promoting a "cause"*: Some organizations focus on a specific area of work, and some services offer the opportunity to develop specialized knowledge for a particular cause. Workers in these services can often be extremely passionate about their field, and can stimulate a similar passion in you.

- *Developing a greater range of skills*: Public sector field work may develop certain skills, but the voluntary sector could broaden your portfolio of skills in tasks such as fundraising, advocacy, community development, research, giving presentations (useful for when you come to job interviews!) or representing the agency, organization or institution at community events. For example, running a group may be easier to achieve in many voluntary sector placements, and sometimes students report that looking at ethical and moral issues can be easier in settings where your role is to advocate against unjust decisions on behalf of clients.

Possible Disadvantages and What to Do?

Many key points about the value of such placements discussed earlier within the commercial sector also apply to the voluntary sector:

- You may feel isolated as the only "social service worker."

- Working in teams and the need for clarity around your role, the way it is different from the roles of colleagues, and you're your experience will be evaluated.

Resolving these issues is described in detail above. The voluntary sector may have certain specific issues to consider in addition, the main one being:

- *Funding*: Most voluntary organizations are trapped in short term contracts, and funding for projects or programs can often be challenging. This can have certain advantages for you as a student in that it will show you how people deal with the realities of working in an uncertain world, but obviously this can create its own pressure, particularly for staff. When you are offered a placement in a voluntary sector service, it is always useful to gain some background knowledge of how the agency, organization or institution is funded. Funding needs to be secure for at least as long as you will be there, and it is your Field Work Supervisor's responsibility to reflect on the impact which these issues may have on you.

Transferability of Skills

It is always interesting to interview graduates after completing their field placement because sometimes students have answered questions by relating what they haven't done rather than focusing on what they have accomplished. A human service candidate said:

> "I've not done assessments."

While another said:

> *"I have developed sound assessment skills and am able to gather information and analyze this effectively to form assessments. I'm not particularly familiar at this stage with the documentation used in your agency but I've used a range of documentation and I'm confident that I can quickly become familiar with the documentation you use."*

Which would you go for? Neither student has had a public sector placement but one has a positive attitude and has reflected on transferring skills, while the other has a negative, defeatist attitude.

While it can be beneficial to have some public sector field experience when applying for employment, it is not essential. Students have been able to secure employment in public sector (if they wanted this) where they had experienced voluntary or commercial settings, even those students who are competing against candidates with public sector experience. Gaining mastery over social service work skills are what matters and these can be developed by students (with the right approach) in any setting. To make the most of every field placement opportunity, focus on your skill development, not the context in which this is taking place.

Placement in the Public Sector

There are a number of advantages to a public sector field placement. Students have indicated that completing a field placement in a government mandated agency allowed them to gain knowledge and skills that they believe placed them in a better position when competing for employment. For instance, students who were placed with the municipal social services department were able to gain an understanding of the different levels of government; the associated procedures and pressures with being a part of a mandated public agency; how programs and services are funded; they were able to gain valuable experience in being able to assess clients for financial aid eligibility; and learn about different agencies within their community. However, some students have indicated that they had limited opportunity to provide advocacy to clients and families or use clinical intervention strategies taught throughout their program of study.

There is no doubt that the "perfect" field placement experience would include all three settings; public, commercial and voluntary sectors. The worst thing you could possibly do is to go into whatever placement you are offered with a negative "I wish I was somewhere else" attitude. To assume that a public sector experience equals a good experience is not accurate. In fact sometimes the opposite can be true as staff in the public sector struggle to provide the time and support that student's need. Some students felt that by having opportunities in the voluntary sector let them do what they perceived as "real social service work." Typically, students felt that placements within voluntary sector settings had supported them to build up their skills and knowledge and that this effectively prepared them for public sector work.

SUMMARY

Field placements are now offered in a wide variety of settings. Every placement has advantages and disadvantages. Making the most of your field placement is critical, and it is your responsibility to identify which skills you will be able to transfer to future roles.

WHAT ARE FIELD WORK SUPERVISORS LOOKING FOR?

When people apply for employment, they work hard to make sure their application reflects the roles and responsibilities identified in the job description. When you're "applying" for a placement, you often have no idea where you might be placed or what you are applying for. We recognize that this can make completing your field placement request form difficult. The purpose of this chapter is to assist you in identifying what Field Work Supervisors are looking for in students.

Many of the students have been unclear about what Field Work Supervisors are looking for in a student at the start of a placement. Others, who have thought they were clear, have misunderstood what Field Work Supervisors are really looking for in students.

Students often think that Field Work Supervisors are looking for experienced students with a certain level of pre-existing skills. Having worked with a large number of Field Work Supervisors throughout the years, the following list details what Field Supervisors are truly searching for:

- enthusiasm
- commitment to learning
- willingness to accept feedback, guidance and advice
- willingness to take initiative
- willingness to make mistakes and learn from them
- open attitude
- questioning approach
- motivation
- interest in the work of the placement
- commitment to service and the values of your profession
- willingness to challenge themselves and others
- honesty
- willingness to reflect on issues in supervision
- commitment to exploring and challenging their own emotions and values
- basic (foundation) skills in communication, team working and "people skills"

SUMMARY

Field Work Supervisors can be just as apprehensive about placements as students are. They want to make sure the placement match is a "good fit." It's useful for students to be aware of what Field Work Supervisors are looking for – generally an enthusiastic student who is open and willing to learn. Students who demonstrate that they are a good fit in making requests for placements and in informal meetings are likely to find it easier to get a placement.

KEY LEARNING POINTS: SECTION B

- Placement matching is a complex process – each College will have its own process.

- You need to make sure that you understand the process of placement matching in your College and that you work within it.

- Your field placement request form, your cover letter, your resume and your professional development portfolio are crucial. You need to spend time on these and get it right!

- Field Coordinators and Field Work Supervisors are looking for students who are enthusiastic. They want to work with students who have potential, but they don't expect you to be already highly skilled.

- While students may have very clear ideas about where they want to go on placement, keeping an open mind is important.

- Placements can be provided in a range of settings, each of which will have a range of advantages and disadvantages.

- You need to approach whatever field placement opportunity you are offered with a positive approach.

- You get out of field placement learning what you put into it!

PREPARING FOR A PLACEMENT AND GETTING STARTED

Preparing for placement and setting the right 'tone' from the outset is undoubtedly the most important aspect of a successful placement. Remember the **4P rule**:

Poor Preparation will Lead to a Poor Placement

Effective Preparation will certainly build the odds in favour of a success.

You have some courses on preparing for field placement as part of your in school curriculum . Make sure that you attend these and embrace the learning to prepare fully.

CLARIFYING YOUR LEARNING GOALS

11

What are your learning goals? This is a potentially difficult question to answer when you don't know what you don't know! Answering this may seem overwhelming, and for many students it may feel like the first part of a test where the boundaries and the expected answers are unclear.

It is important for students to complete the activities included in this chapter. These activities can help you to identify your learning goals and set the agenda for learning. This is part of the process of preparing effectively for your placement as you are likely to be asked about your learning goals at both the informal and formal meetings, as well as in your initial supervision sessions with your Field Work Supervisor.

Bring and Buy

This is a straightforward activity and it involves you working on a list of what you are bringing to the placement. This might include experiences, skills, knowledge, and characteristics. You should also create a list of what you want to "buy," for instance, what do you want to get from the placement?

Bring	Buy

This exercise has a number of objectives:

- It is much easier for most students to identify with the exercise rather than a more abstract question about your learning goals.

- Thinking about what you have to bring to the placement is about valuing your prior experiences; completing this exercise typically makes students feel more "skilled" at the start of their placements.

- The phrase "learning goals" can seem like the Field Work Supervisors role is to teach you things which you do not already know, whereas the idea that you have a set of items you want to "buy" sounds more like you are an active adult learner. You are in this for a set of unique, personal, professional and valid reasons, and it is your responsibility to "buy" what you need from the placement.

Confidence Checklist

An alternative approach to identifying your learning goals is to work on a "confidence checklist". The idea is that you ask your Field Work Supervisor to help you identify the key things you will need to do in your field placement. The following in an example of a confidence checklist:

Issue / Task	Confident	Not Confident	Action required	Achieved
Using a reflective journal				
Meeting new people				
Answering the telephone				
Using a computer				
Written communication				
Speaking up /taking initiative				
Approaching a supervisor				
Documentation				
Completing an assessment/referral form				
Taking initiative with tasks				
Working with other professionals				
Making effective use of supervision				

The list of tasks could be endless and you need to work with your Field Work Supervisor to prioritize key areas.

You then work down the list checking whether this is an area which you are confident in or not. Alternatively, you could score each area on a scale of 1 to 10 – 10 being very confident, 1 being very unsure. You can then work together with your Field Work Supervisor to devise actions to support you as required. The checklist may be referred to in supervision later on in the placement. Actions can be reviewed and you might then re-score yourself in each area. Some students feel less confident as the placement progresses and they realize the extent of what they need to achieve to complete each task (as demonstrated in the theory of cognitive dissonance – see Chapter 15).

Specific Learning Needs for Some Students

Social service work is a values led profession and everyone involved in social work field placement learning will want to make sure that all students have equal opportunities. Equal opportunities are not about "treating everybody the same," it is about applying anti-oppressive practice, recognizing and responding to diversity and addressing peoples' unique and specific needs and goals.

Many students will experience specific barriers to field placement. Barriers include issues which you have faced in your personal history or ongoing personal experiences outside of your placement. Students may have specific health issues, learning difficulties or disabilities. Whatever specific issues you might face, it is important to be open about them with your Field Work Supervisor and Faculty Advisor as early as possible, as this will enable your Field Work Supervisor to ensure that the placement meets your needs and goals. It is important, however, to remember that your Field Work Supervisors role is to support you so far as you need that support to access the placement, but they are not there to support, give advice or "social service work" you in any way.

You will also need to talk to your Field Work Supervisor about how much information about your specific learning goals you will need to share with the staff.

Your Faculty Advisor or Field Coordinator will not share personal information about you without your permission, but sometimes some students may need to share personal information which could influence their work performance. Issues such as bereavement or abuse could mean that working in certain situations create extra (but not impossible) challenges.

Students with Disabilities / Health Needs

A social work placement can be an intimidating and difficult experience for disabled and non-disabled students alike (Parker, 2004), perhaps even more so for college students as this is often a student's first exposure to the world of "real" social service work. For students with disabilities, the decision to disclose information about your accommodation requirements may not be the real issue, but you may face certain challenges over the assumptions people may make about your learning goals and needs in relation to your accommodation requests. Students frequently report feeling anxious about other peoples' reactions following a disclosure and have expressed concern about what to report on placement forms.

Self-disclosure of "hidden" disabilities can be a real challenge for many students who face specific barriers in their field placement. Some students may fear that disclosing certain difficulties, such as dyslexia, might affect the range of opportunities they are offered or how they are treated while on placement. And yet, "non-disclosure could lead to adverse comments about grammar, spelling and sentence structure, making disclosure both more necessary and more difficult" (Phillips, 1998).

Self-disclosure is important if you need to have a form of accommodation at your practic-uum site. If the construction of social work competence and the self-image of many social workers are built upon "coping" as Phillips (1998) suggests, then self-disclosure of difficul-ties may be important to challenge the view that people with disabilities cannot cope. If you have specific needs, then individualized and effective support is not something which placements provide to enable you to "manage." It is your right to receive support. For example, the limitation of technology and time is not your issue if access to placement opportunities is viewed in this light (Furness & Gilligan, 2004).

The Best Practice Guide states: "Disclosure should be made to the course and the place-ment as early as possible. Disclosure of disability is a matter of personal choice and it is important that you consider the valid reasons for and against disclosure. However, if your course or placement is not aware of your disability, it may not be able to make reasonable adjustments to help you" (Wray, Fell, Stanley, Manthorpe, & Coyne, 2005).

The term "reasonable adjustments" in the above quotation, is important. The Ontario Human Rights Code (2002) guarantees the right to equal treatment in education, without discrimination on the ground of disability, as part of the protection for equal treatment and this protection applies to elementary, secondary and all post-secondary institutions (Ontario Human Rights Commission, 2002). Therefore, all students are legally entitled to expect reasonable accommodations, both in the college environment and on field placement. This means that placement providers, supervisors and Field Work Supervisor will need to be creative in the learning and evaluation methods utilized and make reasonable accommoda-tions to meet your needs if this applies to you (Ontario Human Rights Commission, 2002).

If you have a disability, your Faculty Advisor and Field Work Supervisor will want to negoti-ate with you about what accommodations you will require. They will also want to explore with you how the learning opportunities that are provided and the evaluation methods to be utilized, may need to be adapted (for example, the provision of information in large print or Braille). You may need to ensure that certain equipment or facilities are available for you if you have a disability or a specific health need. For example, you may need a refrigerator to keep medication cold, you may need a quiet room to take a short rest in, or you may need to ensure that an amplified telephone or mobile phone is available. The majority of colleges have a Learning Support Services branch that will be able to advise and assist with this. Some students may have a learning strategist to assist them. If this applies to you, you will need to advise your Field Work Supervisor about the extent of their role. All of this shows how important placement planning and preparation is. You will also need to discuss with your Field Work Supervisor how much information (if any) about your health and support accommodations should be shared with others in the setting.

The following checklist is helpful in considering some of the issues which may help you to ensure your placement agreement meets your goals if you have a disability or a specific health need:

√ You have the right to be respected for your dignity and worth and to contribute to your community.

√ You have the right to equal treatment in service and education without discrimination because of disability.

√ You should be able to access reasonable accommodations to ensure the maximum amount of appropriate learning opportunities are available to you on field placement.

√ If you have a learning strategist, it is important to make sure everyone is familiar with their role.

√ You should have access to any necessary technology and equipment.

√ Challenge any barrier within yourself or the placement setting which blocks your ability to function, participate and develop.

Cultural Needs

It is important to consider and discuss any specific cultural needs. For example, is there a room which could be used by you if you need to pray? If the placement setting has set holidays around Christmas and Easter, remember that these are Christian festivals. You have the right to celebrate other cultural festivals such as Eid (Festival of Sacrifice) or Hanukkah (Festival of Lights). During festivals which might involve fasting, you may need to discuss adapting working hours. Make sure you discuss any specific needs you might have with your Field Work Supervisor. They will be keen to understand your needs and to ensure they negotiate appropriate arrangements with you.

Other Specific Needs

You may have specific needs relating to other issues or experiences. You need to think these through and reflect on how you feel they could be addressed in the field placement environment. Discuss any issues with your Field Work Supervisor as early as possible.

SUMMARY

Identifying your learning goals requires you to be proactive in considering what you want out of the placement and what you need in order to achieve your objectives. Specific needs such as health issues or learning difficulties can be planned for in a positive way if self-disclosure is possible for you.

DO YOUR HOMEWORK!

12

We do hope that the heading of this chapter doesn't come across as too childish. Before your placement starts you need to research the placement setting, the clients that are served by the agency, organization or institution and the geographical area. No one is expecting you to research and know everything before you start the placement – you won't be expected to know everything by the time your placement ends! However, if you do research, your enthusiasm, commitment and interest will shine bright. It will help you to make a positive impression with the practicum site as you will have some knowledge on which to build and have shown that you can take initiative.

You should try to:

- locate and explore the website of your agency, organization and institutions (if they have one)
- research the mission statement, objectives and values of the agency, organization or institution
- research the geographical area – the internet has lots of useful information about demographics of particular areas
- find out about the clients served by the agency (you could ask your Faculty Advisor or another faculty for advice)
- ask your Field Work Supervisor (or on site supervisor if applicable) to direct you towards any reading you could do in preparation for the placement

Any research you do will need to be placed into context once you start placement, but this research will help you to think through any questions you have and may help you to clarify or add to your learning goals.

The following letter from a student demonstrates the benefit of doing your homework.

"I completed my social service worker diploma part time and was sponsored by my employer – the CAS. It took three years to complete and involved two field placements – one in the first year and the other in the second year. I had two very different placement experiences.

I really had no idea what I wanted to do for my first placement, other than that it should be something completely different from my own workplace. At that time, I was doing supervised access visits with the CAS. I had several discussions with my Field Placement Co-coordinator, who was very helpful. She suggested a placement with a residential facility for young offenders. I would be working with young adults female offenders, aged between 18 and 25.

Having accepted the placement, it was important to me to gain a basic understanding of the services provided to youth that I would be working with – issues around substance misuse and the youth justice system. The main sources of my research were government websites, but I also found a number of informative websites just by Googling "drug and alcohol misuse" and "youth justice" in Ontario.

There were a number of challenges in this placement; by its very nature, the environment of a young offender can be very oppressive. How was I to gain the clients trust? How was I going to support the clients to address their drug or alcohol problem while they were likely feeling stressed and anxious by their situation? My previous research and discussions with my Field Work Supervisor and other staff members helped me to find ways around the issues.

Just a few weeks before my second placement was due to start, I decided it would be better to stay with my employer and use the placement time as an opportunity to learn and understand the other units I would be working with as a qualified social service worker. It was an opportunity for me to do work with my current employer within a different unit.

I needed less preparation for this placement as I was staying within my own employer and already had an understanding of the policies, procedures and paperwork involved.

There was really only one challenge with this placement, but it was a major one – and that was to be recognized as a student and not as a regular member of the team. This was very much a struggle throughout the placement due to short staffing and the many changes following a re-organization. I have to acknowl-

continued...

edge that my own need to be seen as a "team player" created a guilt in me that caused me to ignore my student status too. I carried a significantly reduced case load, but it was still twice and at times three times the size, greater than other students had.

From my experiences, I would strongly advise against undertaking a placement within one's own employer even if it means working in a different position that you have already done. I feel that it is extremely important to be seen as a student and equally important to see yourself as a student. From my own experience, this is virtually impossible to achieve.

In both placements, perhaps the most useful tool was a field placement log I produced to show my days on placement and on study leave or annual leave. While this needed slight adjustments as I was going along, by having my schedule clearly planned, I could ensure that I completed the placement and all coursework on time over the placement period. I gave a copy to my onsite supervisor at work, my Field Work Supervisor and Faculty Advisor so that everyone could follow and monitor my progress.

I would also strongly advise any student to do your homework by researching and obtaining as much information about the placement prior to commencement. It certainly helped me in my first placement to have a basic understanding of the youth justice system and the substance misuse services available.**

– Anonymous SSW Student

SUMMARY

Undertaking some research in preparation for your placement will be valuable to you and will enhance your learning. It will also demonstrate your enthusiasm to your Field Work Supervisor.

GROUND RULES AND BOUNDARIES

13

It will be clear from what you have read so far that clarity about ground rules and boundaries in field placement are essential. The success of a placement will rely on you agreeing and following some clear ground rules and boundaries at the beginning of the placement.

Ground Rules

Part of an effective learning environment is being clear about ground rules. Whenever you go on any training course in your future career, you will start with agreeing to some form of ground rules. In a field placement, ground rules are essential. No ground rule should be left "unwritten," and no assumption can be made that you understand professional ground rules – these are not always obvious even to people who have experience in the field. Your Field Work Supervisor is likely to spend time with you early in your placement establishing ground rules such as:

- confidentiality
- appropriate challenging
- professional behaviour
- expectations with regard to dress
- use of cell phones
- relationships with staff members
- relationships and boundaries with clients
- use of the internet at work
- normal working hours and breaks

This list is not exhaustive but certainly highlights the important areas you should consider. Within different practicum settings, staff members may have different ground rules about these areas, so it is vital to discuss these with your Field Work Supervisor as early as possible to make sure that you are clear about organizational culture and expectations. Students do not want to alienate colleagues by breaking their rules or not respecting their norms or organizational culture.

"Ground rules directly reflect social work values and this can be made explicit in setting them up" (Atherton, 2006). Taking initiative to establish ground rules at the start of your placement will help you to demonstrate your understanding of, and commitment to, social work values right from the start of the placement.

A collaborative approach to establishing ground rules actually helps in promoting a safe learning environment for you as this discussion will ensure that you are clear as to exactly what expectations there are of you.

Boundaries with Staff and Colleagues

Sometimes boundaries in field placement relationships can become blurred for some students. This could be the boundary between you and a staff member, or between you and your Field Work Supervisor. Essentially, what you need to remember is that the relationships you build with your colleagues and your Field Work Supervisor (and supervisor where relevant) are professional relationships and therefore professional boundaries need to be in place. As hard as it may sound, you are not there to make friends and you have a job to do (basically, successfully meeting the program learning outcomes so that you pass your placement), and that forms the basis of your relationships during this time.

This is not to say, of course, that boundaries can't change when the field placement relationship ends. While the placement is in progress, however, you have to consider the boundaries of your relationships with your colleagues as they are likely to take part in your evaluation, at least informally. If difficulties arise during your placement, it is also really important that you do not draw staff members into these unnecessarily. This could have an impact upon other people's well-being and workload, the staff morale, and ultimately on your evaluation for these reasons (see Chapter 29 for more detail on what to do in these situations).

Boundaries with Clients

For many social service work students, it may be the first time you have worked in a professional capacity with vulnerable people. In your program of study, you are likely to have already covered professional conduct, anti-oppressive practice and communication skills, linked to the OCSWSSW Code of Ethics and Standards of Practice. However, on placement, it may be important for you to consider how you will establish, maintain and review the effectiveness of the ways in which you maintain your professional boundaries with clients.

Consider some of the following key questions in relation to your professional relationships with clients. Would you, for example:

- Take a child to school for a parent who is struggling?
- Give a client your home or personal mobile phone number?
- Text a client from your cell to confirm that they can make an appointment?
- Talk to a client about your personal circumstances?

- Allow a client to request you as a friend on a social networking site?
- Take a client for a "pub lunch"?
- Lend money to a client (e.g., for bus fare)?
- Call a client outside of normal business hours to see if they are okay?
- Help a client with practical tasks during a home visit, such as cleaning up a messy living area?
- Accept gifts from a client when you come to say goodbye at the end of your placement?

SUMMARY

Ground rules and professional boundaries are an essential aspect of all social service work practice. Your colleagues in your placement are there to support you, but may also take part in some of your evaluation. Ground rules and boundaries with clients should be carefully negotiated at the outset of your engagement with people and kept under review. SSW students must comply with Code of Conduct and Standards of Practice outlined by the OCSWSSW. Similarly, DSW and CYW students need to comply with their respective Code of Conduct and Standards of Practice outlined by their regulatory body.

ORIENTATION

14

There are two components to an orientation:

- Orientation package: what you are provided with at the start of the placement
- Orientation program: what you actually do for the first part of your placement

Do not be afraid to ask questions, for instance, how to work the photocopier, or where the washroom is! Even when you may be worried about asking something you think may be perceived as "stupid," remember that everyone has questions! There really is no such thing during orientation as a silly question. We often learn more by getting it wrong at first, and keep in mind that the staff members will empathize, support, and help you settle in. Asking questions during your orientation (and indeed throughout the placement) will not be viewed negatively – in fact, the opposite is often true. I have been involved in a number of field placement situations where staff members have indicated negatively that "the student never asks any questions...they just don't seem interested." That said, it could be viewed negatively if you ask the same questions over and over again, so do make a note of information you are finding difficult to remember.

Orientation Package

You are likely to be provided with a significant amount of information at the beginning of the placement – which forms your orientation package. Sometimes there is so much information provided within the orientation package that it can feel overwhelming! Students are often keen to "get on with the job" when they first start placement. Some students focus on trying to meet the key roles from day one. However, learning is a staged process and there can be a great deal for you to learn before you can begin to take on "work" within the placement setting. You will need to read the information you are provided with as this will set the context for your practice, for example, it will help you to understand the policies and procedures of the agency, organization or institution in which you are placed.

It may be useful to make notes in relation to your readings to help you remember. You should also make a note of where you can find information again for future reference. For example, you might need to refer back to a specific process at a later stage when you are working with a particular client.

You may feel anxious to "actually get on with something," but it is vital that you work through all of the information you are provided with during your orientation and that you ask questions to clarify when necessary. It is widely acknowledged that you must have a clear understanding of your practicum site to be able to demonstrate competence in meeting the program learning outcomes. For example, Furness & Gilligan (2004) state that:

Competence = ability + knowledge + understanding

You can, therefore, be successful on your field placement if you have developed your knowledge and understanding at the start of the placement. The preliminary reading you do is "doing something" – it is doing something very important. If you skip this in an attempt to move straight into "doing" or active practice, you are likely to find yourself unprepared.

Orientation Program

Formal and informal orientation programs will help you to learn some of the essential components of agency, organizational or institutional practice and help you to become familiar with the staff and help clarify your role. Often many Field Work Supervisors and Faculty Advisors believe a two week orientation period is appropriate. However, as you are coming to the field placement as a learner rather than a new worker, activities which are traditionally seen as part of an orientation can be spread across the entire placement.

> **"**I had an excellent orientation which I haven't had in other placements. I can see now, on reflection, how an orientation really shapes your whole placement.**"**

Orientations programs should allow for a staged approach to learning with options for information to be revisited and reviewed (Mullins, 2005).

The importance of the orientation period cannot be underestimated. It sets the tone for the placement – if your orientation is thorough, you will feel valued and welcomed by the practicum site. The orientation should help you to prepare effectively for your field placement and help you to feel more comfortable about your roles.

You may be asked to provide feedback on your orientation at the end of the two weeks, so do take time to consider what you have gained from each learning opportunity and whether you feel any more time needs to be spent on certain reading, visits or activities. This shows that you are taking initiative in your learning and that you are able to identify your own areas for development right at the start of the placement.

Making the Most of Your Orientation and Creating a Good Impression

You need to take a proactive approach to your orientation. Work through the information you are provided with and make sure you understand it, engage in all the opportunities you are offered and reflect on your learning.

Many students can feel overwhelmed with information during the first few days and weeks and certainly it's likely that your learning curve will be very steep during your orientation period. The people you meet will be forming their first impressions of you and since these are the people you will be working with throughout the placement, the impressions you create are important. People are more likely to open up a range of learning opportunities for you if they have a good impression of you.

If you are not great with names you might find it difficult to recall everyone's name while you are taking on so much new information. Using people's names can create a good impression. If you are in an office setting, it can be really useful to draw a diagram of the office layout and jot down names by desks. Alternatively, try jotting information next to names to help you remember who is who.

Students often find themselves incredibly tired by taking in so much information and making the transition from college to the work environment. However, if you can find the time and energy to jot a few notes at the end of every day, it will really help you to maximize your learning from orientation.

"Upon starting my final field placement opportunity within Adult Services, a new area of practice for me, I was presented with a very comprehensive orientation package which covered the first four weeks of my placement. This involved accompanying my Field Work Supervisor on visits as well as other practitioners and spending time in different areas of the service in order to familiarize myself with its components.

Initially, I felt this was a little excessive. The first four weeks had been planned out for me and it felt that I wasn't spending any time on direct practice myself. With my first assignment looming, I became somewhat anxious as I would need to demonstrate that I was meeting the program learning outcomes with clients. I was becoming impatient and was eager to "hit the ground running" as this is what I had been used to in Children's Services. I felt somewhat overwhelmed with the thought that I was effectively wasting time learning all of this new information I may never need and, to some extent, I also felt deskilled by the orientation process.

I met with my Field Work Supervisor, who was extremely supportive, and allowed me to appreciate the value of this experience and to take time to absorb all I was being privileged to observe. In supervision discussion, my Field Work Supervisor helped me to recognize that the skills which I already had needed to be transferred into a new area where the pace and nature of practice was different. I began to

continued...

understand that having the luxury of this time to just absorb and take in what was new allowed me to fit the pieces of the puzzle together. This discussion helped me to recognize that my anxiety was getting in the way of my learning. Subsequently, I made sure that I was active within the orientation, getting to know various people within the different services in order to develop a network of support which would prove invaluable throughout the rest of my placement.

I ensured that I took time at the end of each day to jot down the key learning points in order to reflect upon them, which proved invaluable towards the end of my placement when I was required to write an analysis of my learning and practice.

Before long I was allocated cases and was soon able to practice with more confidence than I would have if I hadn't had the orientation that was in place for me. I managed to reach each of the program learning outcomes. During my direct practice I was able to reflect upon and utilize the knowledge I had gained throughout my orientation and build on the networks I had made.

On reflection, my orientation was extremely positive and valuable to my learning. Therefore, if you are offered an orientation period my advice would be to endeavor to embrace this opportunity as I am sure you will find it valuable. Take this opportunity to be enquiring and visit areas of the service that you feel would enhance your knowledge and ultimately your practice. **"**

– Anonymous SSW Student

SUMMARY

Your orientation is really important as it sets the tone for the rest of the placement. Getting the most out of orientation involves being pro-active in studying the information you are given and in identifying and opening yourself to the learning opportunities you are offered and reflecting on the learning you have achieved.

KEY LEARNING POINTS: SECTION C

- Preparing for placement is important. If effective preparation does not take place, the placement probably will not go well. It is partly up to you to make sure that the placement works for you from the start.

- You should spend time reflecting on your learning goals and objectives.

- It is essential that you share your learning goals with your Field Work Supervisor.

- If you have any specific learning needs you should share these with your Field Work Supervisor so that any necessary adjustments can be made.

- The more research you do prior to starting your placement the better equipped you will be.

- Ground rules and boundaries are an essential to having a positive experience.

- The more proactive you are in your orientation, the better the impression you will create.

TAKING RESPONSIBILITY FOR YOUR OWN LEARNING

D

While there may be a place for some specific teaching and learning in your relationship with your Field Work Supervisor, they are not expected to be proficient with a chalkboard! The teaching aspect of their role is much more about facilitating your learning. You will already have learned about key aspects of human service work through your time in your program of study. The Field Work Supervisor's role is essentially about supporting you to apply course work to practice and to facilitate your learning about the environments. Field placement learning is always a two way process and you need to take a proactive approach to your own learning. This section will help you to explore how you can do just that.

ADULT LEARNING THEORY

15

In order to maximize your learning on placement, it is worthwhile for you to understand the main theories and principles of adult learning. Understanding how you learn best will empower you to take initiative and enjoy the learning experiences and opportunities which your placement will offer you.

Basic Principles of Adult Learning

- ### *The Law of Exercise*

Adults learn best when they take part in the activity they are learning about. The law of exercise basically means that the more opportunities a person has to engage in an activity, the more they will learn about it. Repetition is the mother of all skills (Smith, 2006) and practice makes perfect sums it up really well! This is why field placement is at the heart of your program and is required to become qualified and competent in the field.

- ### *The Law of Association*

Adults learn best by adding to, or building on, previously acquired knowledge. If we have already had an experience and we have a similar or related experience, then we are more likely to learn from it. The more we can associate new experiences and learning with something we have previously learned, the more likely we are to learn from the new experience.

- ### *The "Need to Know" Motivation*

Adults always learn something more effectively if they want to or need to learn it. The attitude of "what's the point?" will render us less likely to learn or retain the learning if it is not relevant to what we are doing. This could mean that sometimes you might learn better about local resources, theoretical approaches or the legal framework when you need to apply your learning to specific areas of your work.

- ### *The Need to be Self-directing*

Adults need to take responsibility for what they learn. We learn best when we are directing our own learning. Many of the processes in field placement build on this principle – for example, asking you to identify your own learning goals and objectives and to engage fully in devising your own learning contract.

- ### *The Willingness and Readiness to Learn*

Similar to the self-directing principle noted above, if someone is not ready to learn and puts up barriers or roadblocks, then no matter how good the experience of learning or the quality of the teaching or facilitation, the person will not be able to learn effectively. This is why issues outside of your placement need to be dealt with proactively so that they do not interfere with your field placement. Your readiness to learn from your placement is also likely to be guided by you wanting to complete the placement and ultimately to qualify as a professional to work in the field.

- ### *Learning Empowerment*

If the relationship between the Field Work Supervisor and the student is seen as one where the Field Work Supervisor is the full container and the student is the empty vessel, the full value of the field placement will not be realized. The Field Work Supervisor's role is to support students in acquiring information, knowledge and skills. Teaching is an important method used to empower professionals (Rose & Black, 1985). Mutuality is critical for being able to empower throughout the teaching process: the Field Work Supervisor learns from the students themselves what their preferred solutions are and what they need to know. Likewise, from settings in which empowerment is realized, the Field Work Supervisor also learns how to plan and activate empowerment enhancing opportunities for students. The majority of professionals in human service agencies, organizations or institutions should be familiar with the concept of empowerment and how it is used.

- ### *The Learning Environment*

The situation in which we learn is paramount – we need to feel safe to learn and confident to learn. The Field Work Supervisor and the staff at your placement site should work to create a safe and trusting learning environment for you.

- ### *Plateau Learning*

We have all heard the phrase "a steep learning curve." Our learning ebbs and flows, so we will have days when we learn more than others, and some days where we feel we are not learning anything new at all. Having time and space to strengthen learning before taking on new learning is important. Learning curves all need to plateau at some point.

- ### *Lifelong Learning*

Adults continue to learn throughout their lives. We need to recognize that we never stop learning and it is imperative that we never believe that we cannot learn any more. This is the reason why the social service work profession requires ongoing professional development in order to maintain membership with the Ontario College of Social Work and Social Service Workers. The professional standards that guide your work as a Registered Social Service Worker require that you stay current through the Continuing Competence Program. Similarly, other professional organizations will have requirements around ongoing professional development.

- *Positive Learning*

If we receive positive reinforcement about a subject or previously learned experience, we are more likely to retain or learn from it. This reinforces the need for you to seek and to listen to constructive feedback to facilitate your learning.

Theories of Adult Learning

This chapter covers three key theories of adult learning which can help you to understand how to maximize your learning on field placement.

I. Experiential Learning

This theory is sometimes misinterpreted as simply saying that people learn through experience. To some extent this is true, but experiential learning theory stresses that it is not enough for people to have an experience. They won't learn from this unless they spend some time reflecting on the experience. Perhaps the most well-known academic to write about experiential learning is D.A. Kolb.

The following diagram details Kolb's (1984) cycle and how this may apply to your field placement:

Experience
You have a relevant experience in your field placement

Reflection
Following the experience, consider: What happened? How was I feeling when this happened? What was I most aware of throughout and what am I aware of now? What went well?

Conceptualization
Make the linkages to other previous learning by considering: How does this experience link with theory or other courses I have taken? How does that link with other pieces of work I have done? What conclusions could I draw?

Experimentation
Plan how to implement this learning. What might I do differently next time? How will I put that into practice for the future?

This theory of adult learning emphasizes the need to reflect and learn from the many experiences you will have. You won't necessarily learn from the experience unless you follow through the learning cycle in supervision with your Field Work Supervisors and in Integrative Seminars with your Faculty Advisor.

As a student you may feel really "stuck" at certain parts in the learning cycle. For example, you may be able to reflect on an experience and draw conclusions about what you might want to do differently next time, but then continue to feel like you are repeating the same mistakes. In this scenario, you may be getting stuck at the "active experimentation" phase, so with your Field Work Supervisor, you may want to consider this in more detail to develop your skills around conceptualization and considering future alternatives for ways of approaching similar situations. Most Faculty Advisors provide opportunities for conceptualization during the Integrative Seminar.

II. Cognitive Dissonance

Cognitive Dissonance theory was first written in 1957 and is useful in understanding peoples behaviours and motivations (Festinger, 1957). There are essentially four phases identified within cognitive dissonance theory that could be applied to students on field placement.

1. Unconscious Incompetence

During this phase students are asked to do a new task, "we don't know what we don't know." It could be said that we're incompetent or naive but that we are unconscious of this. In a way this is quite a comfortable stage – it could be seen as "blissful ignorance." We don't know that we can't do something. However, as we attempt to undertake the new task, we quickly realize that there is a lot more involved than we think and we move onto stage 2.

2. Conscious Incompetence

During this phase we become aware of what we don't know – we realize that we can't do the new task. This is a very uncomfortable and potentially anxiety provoking stage. Many people are socialized to believe "there's no such word as can't," and within the profession it can be important to give the impression that we are competent and knowledgeable to clients. This can feel somewhat distressing as your performance is being evaluated while on placement. Becoming conscious of our incompetence can be distressing. It is important to understand that these feelings are normal and that it is important part of the learning process.

At this phase, some people decide to compromise the learning – give up on the task. Some people can develop quite sophisticated defence mechanisms to ensure that those around them aren't aware of their "incompetence." Think of the highly developed systems that some adults with literacy difficulties have developed.

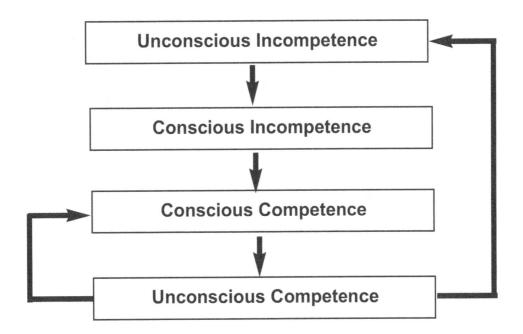

As a student, it is important for you not to give up, to keep asking questions (even if you worry about sounding incompetent – you aren't!), and to feel like you are there to learn. Seek out support and involve yourself in new and useful experiences in order to get through this stage, learn the task and move onto the next stage.

3. Conscious Competence

When we have recently learned a new task we are very aware or conscious about it. Think about that new driver who says to themselves, "check your blind spot, signal, cross over to the next lane" every time they go out in a car! While we may be anxious to ensure we get things right, this is probably the most comfortable and safe stage to be in. We are aware of what we are doing so we are likely to continue to question ourselves and are probably getting it right! The danger is that we will probably, at some point, move onto the next stage.

4. Unconscious Competence

This is where we have become so familiar with the task and confident about our abilities that we almost go into an "automatic pilot" mode. The potentially dangerous aspect of this is that when we are unconscious about something, how do we know that we are still doing it right? Think how many of us (if we are honest) wouldn't pass our driving test today if we just had an examiner sitting in the car on one of our typical drives home. When we are unconscious about something, we slip into bad habits, we take shortcuts – maybe we have actually slipped back to phase one, unconscious incompetence. If we are unconscious, how do we know?

Having an understanding of cognitive dissonance can be very useful in helping your learning. You may be able to acknowledge the need to ask for extra support when you recognize you are in phase two. If you are feeling really confident about a piece of work and then notice that you have missed an important part of the process, then are you in phase four? Considering this theory can help you to assess your stage of competence against your feelings of confidence, and it can support you to demonstrate your ability to show reflective practice in action.

III. Situated Learning Theory

Situated learning theory suggests that learning can only really take place in the context and culture in which the activity normally occurs (i.e., where it is situated). Social interaction is an essential aspect of situated learning, with learners needing to become involved in a "community of practice." As a learner moves from the edge of this community to its centre, they become more active and engaged in their learning. Lave and Wenger (1990) call this process "legitimate peripheral participation." In analyzing situated learning in five different settings, Lave and Wenger found that learners had a gradual acquisition of knowledge and skills as they learned from "experts" in the context of everyday activities (Lave & Wenger, 1990). Clearly situated learning links closely to field placement. You should take every opportunity to become involved and immersed in your host "community of practice" as soon as possible in the placement.

Learning Styles

In addition to adult learning theories, learning styles is another important factor to consider for students preparing for field placement. Honey & Mumford (1982) report that people have different styles of learning; they have developed four different styles and have designed a learning styles questionnaire which identifies which style a person uses most often (Honey & Mumford, 1982). These questionnaires are widely available in many settings; some Field Work Supervisor will do this exercise with you as part of getting to know you at the start of a placement orientation. Some Colleges may ask students to complete a learning styles questionnaire (sometimes referred to as an inventory (i.e., Myers Briggs Type Indicators) at various stages in their program of study including in the Field Preparation course, so you may already be familiar with this exercise.

Four Learning Styles (Honey & Mumford, 1982)

1. Activists

Activists are often open-minded and enthusiastic, and they enjoy new experiences and want to get involved in the here and now. They enjoy getting involved and they learn by "doing." Activists can become bored when an activity stops and will want to quickly move onto the next challenge or activity, rather than dwell on reflection of the last activity.

2. Reflectors

Reflectors do just that! They stand back, reflect, contemplate and consider many perspectives before acting. Reflectors mull things over before reaching a conclusion: they observe, gather information and take plenty of time to think before making a decision.

3. Theorists

Theorists are logical thinkers: they analyze, question and learn step by step in a logical way. Theorists question any new learning and want to ensure it fits and makes sense with their logical approach. Theorists are often perfectionists and do not appreciate a light-hearted approach to a subject or task.

4. Pragmatists

Pragmatists enjoy trying out something new to see if it works in practice. They will often take a problem solving approach to learning and will seek to apply something that they have learned immediately. However, if it doesn't work they are likely not to try the approach again – instead they will try to look for something new to try.

Many colleges and employers in Canada use the Myers Briggs Type Indicator to support people in understanding their learning preferences on scales derived from psychologist Carl Jung's theory of psychological types (Felder & Spurlin, 2005). There are essentially four categories:

Extraverts try things out, focus on the outer world of people whereas **introverts** think things through, focus on the inner world of ideas.

Sensors are practical, detailed-oriented, focus on facts and procedures whereas **intuitive** people are imaginative, concept-oriented, focus on meanings and possibilities.

Thinkers are sceptical, tend to make decisions based on logic and rules whereas **feelers** are appreciative, tend to make decisions based on personal and humanistic considerations.

Judgers set and follow agendas, seek closure even with incomplete data whereas **perceivers** adapt to changing circumstances and resist closure to obtain more data.

The MBTI type preferences can be combined to form 16 different learning style types. For example, one student may be an ESTP (extravert, sensor, thinker, and perceiver) and another may be an INFJ (introvert, intuitive, feeler and judger) (Felder & Spurlin, 2005).

Similar to the Honey-Mumford approach, Myers-Briggs types have similar practical implications for learning on the job, in the classroom and in the field placement. It is useful to have some understanding of these identified styles. It is important to remember that this is a theoretical approach, and most people use different learning approaches and a combination of the above styles in different situations that they encounter. While these learning styles are not scientifically validated, they are used along with other influences to understand how an adult may learn (Honey & Mumford, 1986).

Approaches to Learning

Although they are most well-known for devising learning styles, Honey and Mumford (1986) also emphasize that there are four different approaches to learning. These are different to the styles of learning they discuss. In field placement, references are often made to learning styles and less commonly to approaches to learning. However, understanding the various approaches to learning is useful to consider as part of understanding how you may best learn from your placement. The approaches identified are as follows:

Intuitive Learning

We are not conscious of this, but we are learning by our experience all of the time. If we use the intuitive approach then we are making use of the experiences we have to learn and develop. If this approach is challenged we are able to refer to a variety of detail from our experiences. However, if questioned, the intuitive learner finds it difficult to articulate what they may have learned or how they have learned it.

The Incidental Approach

This generally involves learning by chance from activities that force an individual to engage in some form of reflection of the situation. This reflection can be brought about out of frustration. If something happens to an incidental learner, for example something in their plan goes wrong, they will often reflect over the incident in an unstructured informal way.

This can happen in less formal patterns, such as travelling home, sitting in the backyard or even lying in the bath. Incidental learners often use the "benefit of hindsight" as a way of making sense out of what has happened.

The Retrospective Approach

Similar to the incidental approach, the retrospective learner looks back over what has happened and then goes on to draw a specific conclusion from it. However, people using this approach will also tend to draw lessons from routines and successes. So in effect, they are learning from a diverse range of small and large, positive and negative experiences.

The process looks like this:

The Prospective Approach

This is similar to the above, except that there is another dimension included – this is the dimension of planning. The experience is planned for, set up and then reviewed with conclusions drawn. That means that future plans are seen as learning opportunities as opposed to just merely things to be done. Planned learning experiences are an integral part of your field placement allowing you to be proactive in deciding what learning experiences you would need to meet your learning goals. The sequence in prospective learing is illustrated as follows:

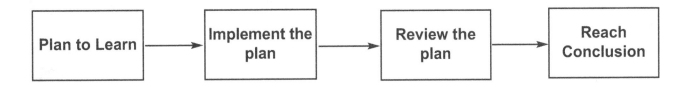

In your field placement, you will need to adopt a prospective approach to learning. You will be expected to identify your learning goals and objectives, to participate in the planning for your learning, to engage in all of the learning activities and opportunities which may be available to you, and to keep your learning meaningful and relevant. You will also be expected to reflect retrospectively on your learning experiences, in supervision with your Field Work Supervisor, in the Integrative Seminar with your Faculty Advisor and probably through keeping a reflective journal required for field placement (see Chapter 16 for more information about reflective learning).

Surface and Deep Approaches to Learning

Approaches to learning describe what students do when they go about learning and why they do it. The terms deep learning and surface learning are widely used concepts in adult learning.

- **Surface approach**
  This approach focuses on acquiring and memorizing information. An uncritical, unquestioning approach is taken to acquiring new knowledge with little reflection. It leads to a superficial retention of information and does not promote an integration of knowledge. Learning could be motivated by external factors such as demands from the placement agency or your assessment requirements.

- **Deep approach**
  This approach involves critically analyzing new ideas and linking them with existing wider knowledge. This approach means the learner will understand and apply the learning to new and different contexts. Deep learning assists with problem solving and making wider analytical connections (Marton & Saljo, 1976).

Don't be a surface learner

Be a deep learner

"*We should not identify the student with a fixed approach to learning…It is the design of learning opportunity that encourages students to adopt a particular approach…Very crudely: deep is good, surface is bad, and we should teach in a way that encourages students to adopt a deep approach; although achieving this is not so easy*" (Houghton, 2004).

Thinking Styles

Danbury (1994) identifies that people have two different thinking styles:

1. Pictorial thinkers have pictorial memories and think visually. They are attracted to visual images such as flowcharts, diagrams, and ecomaps.

2. Verbal thinkers think in words as opposed to pictures and learn best through reading and discussion. Diagrams and imagery will have little meaning for them.

It is worth considering further which style you think you have, to discuss this with your Field Work Supervisor, and to consider adapting some of the methods which you use to suit your preferred style.

SUMMARY

This brief and basic review of theories of adult learning can support your understanding of how adults learn and this be helpful to you in making the most of your field placement. You may well find reflecting on the theories of learning covered in this chapter helpful in evaluating your own learning during the placement.

REFLECTIVE PRACTICE

16

The experiential learning cycle which was discussed in the last chapter shows the importance of you reflecting on all of your experiences on placement in order to learn. Reflective practice regularly comes up on field placement. It is therefore critical that you have a good idea of what the process of reflection really means for you in practice. This will prepare you to have good habits for your working life, rather than reflection being one task which slips because of a busy workload.

There are many definitions for the term reflective practice: reflection means to think about, review or ponder over previous activities because they were effective or there is a need to make sense of them, or the need to evaluate because they may have been ineffective or troublesome (Ranson, 2011). A similar definition is to take the information in relation to your experience, knowledge and skill level shaped through self-assessment, or assessments made by others, analyze it and determine what to do about it in the future. Reflection closes the gap between theory and practice (RNAO, 2012).

Johns (1995) says that reflection is the method of accessing, making sense of, and learning through experience. Reflection is critical for practice professions such as Nurses, Social Service Workers, Child and Youth Workers, and Developmental Service Workers and other human service professionals (Johns, 1995). There are four ways of knowing associated with reflection (Carper, 1978):

Empirical or Scientific • knowing that comes from technical, theoretical knowledge that informs practice • evidence based research that informs professional standards of practice guidelines	**Personal** • knowing that comes from understanding and being aware of self in practice situations • acknowledges the holistic and humanistic nature of working with clients and the feelings they express
Ways of Knowing	
Ethical • knowing that comes from experiencing those conflict situations that result from striving to do what is right and in the best interest of clients	**Aesthetic** • knowing that comes from experience and enables professionals to make a skilled response to an anticipated client situation

The stronger your ability to engage in reflective practices in the field, the greater the congruence between knowledge about practice and what you actually do in the field.

Schön (1987) asserts that there are two types of reflection:

Reflection IN Action

- Thinking ahead – *"Right if that's happened, then I need to..."*
- Analyzing what is happening – *"She's saying that to test me, I think I should..."*
- Storing up experiences for the future – *"I could have dealt with that better, next time I will try..."*
- Being critical – *"That didn't work very well..."*

Reflection ON Action

- Thinking through subsequent to the situation – *"I think I should do this beforehand, so that..."*
- Discussing – *"I will discuss with my Field Work Supervisor..."*
- Reflective journal – *"I will make time at the end of my day to give this more thought..."*

Reflection in Action

Reflection **in** action is the process of reflection when you are engaging in an activity. Essentially it is working and being aware of what you are doing at the same time.

Reflection **in** action is happening all the time – if your mind is on the task! We all know people who are planning their night out while carrying out a task and would all agree that this doesn't constitute good practice. Having your mind on the job is important because not only is it good practice, it also constitutes reflection in action.

While reflection **in** action is good practice and allows you to focus on the here and now, it does have drawbacks. The main problems with reflection in action are:

- You can only see things from your own perspective (*"I think, I feel, I'm not sure..."*)
- You will only have short-term reflection. If your mind is on the task at hand, when the task changes so will your thoughts.

These drawbacks can be addressed by making sure that you also use reflection **on** action.

Reflection on Action

This is the reflecting you do after an event. Reflection **on** action refers to the process of thinking through and perhaps discussing the incident with a colleague or a Field Work Supervisor.

Reflection **on** action is free from urgency and any pressures of the actual event. As such it allows for longer term reflection. You can also ensure that by seeking feedback you use other people's perspectives as part of your reflection.

The main drawback of reflection **on** action is that because of time constraints we tend only to think in this way about more complex or critical work issues. Therefore, in terms of more routine events and work practice, we tend only to "reflect in action." This can lead us to not making much improvement in our daily routines. It is important, therefore, to plan reflection **on** action to ensure that it covers every aspect of practice. Planning to reflect rather than simply doing so when something has gone wrong or has been particularly difficult, is best practice.

When do you reflect?

Reflection BEFORE Action

- emphasizes the importance of reflection in preparation for professional action
- enables the students to identify relevant theory, past experiences, and resources that might be helpful in carrying out the planned action

Reflection IN Action

- involves "thinking on your feet" and calling to mind relevant knowledge, whether scientific or not to enable you to continue a course of action, modify a course of action, call for assistance or stop the action all together

Reflection ON Action

- is reflecting after-the-fact and bringing to mind what was done, the results, and why the results occurred in the way they did, with the view to see how this learning will be used in the future
- is the process of internally examining and exploring an issue of concern triggered by an experience, which creates and clarifies meaning for the individual and results in new learning

Boyd & Fales (1983)

Your Field Work Supervisor and Faculty Advisor might encourage you to develop reflections skills during supervision, and by encouraging you to use reflection before action, reflection in action and reflection on action.

Reflective Journals

Reflective journals are personal records of student learning experiences. Students are typically asked by Faculty Advisors and Field Work Supervisors to record learning-related activities during the field placement.

Most colleges require students to keep reflective journals during their placement; others require students to submit one or two pieces of reflective writing during their placement. Recognizing the value of reflective journals, some Field Work Supervisors ask students to keep one even if this is not a program requirement. Even when you are not asked to keep a reflective journal, it is strongly recommended that you keep one because reflective writing can be a great source of learning. According to Sinclair (2006):

> Some students might benefit from keeping an unstructured reflective journal, as I have. By getting into a regular habit of writing for a few minutes without stopping, I have got a useful record of my own reflections and a way into the more formal writing I am expected to do as a student.

Logs, Diaries and Reflective Journals

Documentation of hours and what students do on field placement is typically a requirement of field placement in any program of study. Most colleges require students to keep records in the form of a log, a journal or a diary. Each method records activities differently.

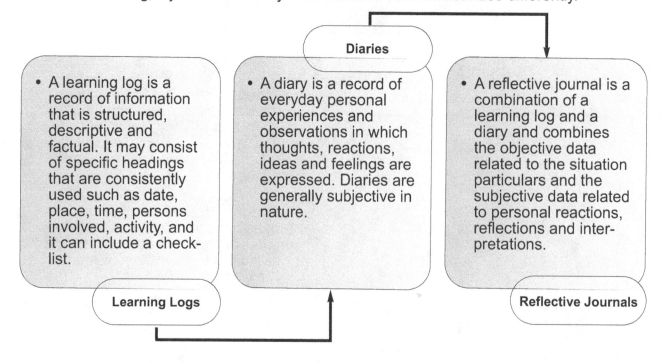

Diaries

- A learning log is a record of information that is structured, descriptive and factual. It may consist of specific headings that are consistently used such as date, place, time, persons involved, activity, and it can include a checklist.

- A diary is a record of everyday personal experiences and observations in which thoughts, reactions, ideas and feelings are expressed. Diaries are generally subjective in nature.

- A reflective journal is a combination of a learning log and a diary and combines the objective data related to the situation particulars and the subjective data related to personal reactions, reflections and interpretations.

Learning Logs

Reflective Journals

Keeping a reflective journal may seem like an inconvenience at first, but it will help you to:

- focus in more detail on significant learning experiences
- provide you with evidence showing that you are meeting the program learning outcomes
- enable you to look back on your learning and be able to track your growth
- help you to identify your skills, knowledge, application of learning, as well as support you in identifying your learning needs more specifically
- help you to identify and provide evidence of your skills and abilities for your evaluation
- assist you in offering more effective interventions for clients
- reflect and learn from feedback you have received to develop your practice

Sometimes students know just how they want to formulate or structure their writing. Some programs of study provide guidance on how they want a student to produce a reflective journal. Some students, however, look for guidance on how to keep a reflective journal. You may find the following model useful in deciding how to set up your reflective journal:

D-I-E-P Formula (RMIT, 2006):

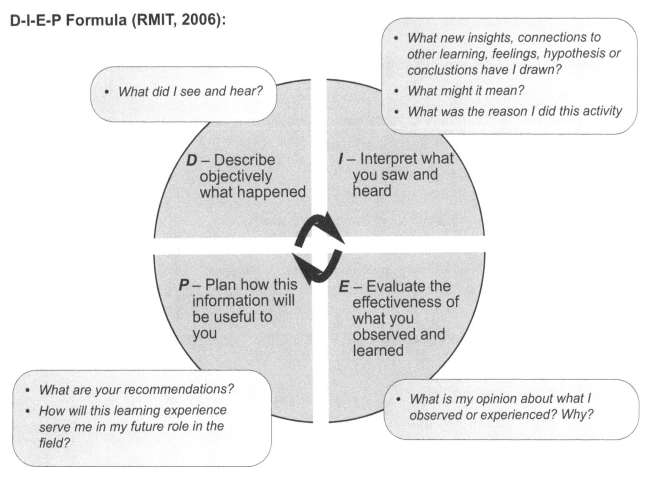

Applying the cycle of experiential learning is another model student's use to guide their reflective journal entries (Ranson, 2011):

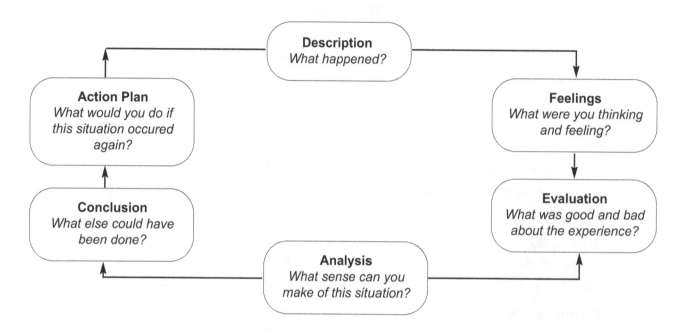

Other students find the following framework useful:

- Date of event:
- Provide a *brief* summary of the event:
- What did you learn from the experience?
- What did you feel *you* did well and why?
- What theories and knowledge did you apply?
- What would you do differently in the future and why?

Students go through a number of stages when writing reflective journals or learning logs. The models presented outline the stages or processes somewhat differently, yet with similar approaches and outcomes. The essence of these models is to provide students with a fundamental method to create a reflective journal and learning log entries.

Method for Creating a Reflective Journal (RMIT, 2006; Johnson, n.d.):

I. Write, record

a) Describe the situation (the learning experience and the context)
b) Who was involved with the situation?
c) What did they have to do with the situation?

II. Reflect, think about

a) What are your reactions?

b) What are your feelings?

c) What are the good and the not so good aspects of the situation?

d) What you have learned?

III. Analyze, explain, gain insight

a) What was really going on?

b) What sense can you make of the situation?

c) Can you integrate theory into the experience/situation (practice)?

d) Can you demonstrate an improved awareness and self-development because of the situation?

IV. Conclusions

a) What can be concluded in a general and specific sense from this situation/experience and the analysis you have undertaken?

V. Personal action plan

a) What are you going to do differently in this type of situation next time?

b) What steps are you going to take on the basis of what you have learned?

The key to reflective journals and learning logs is to track progression over a period of time and to "gain a sense of achievement" (Dalhousie University, n.d.).

Whether you use one of these models or methods for writing a reflective journal or you develop one of your own, the main component is to ensure that you produce more than simply a description of an event – this is a narrative. A reflective account makes it truly personal to you and enhances your learning.

> **"**I have recently completed two of the field placements that are required for my program of study. Both placements have been in residential settings. The first one was in a home for children with learning disabilities and the other one was in a home for older people. I will admit that neither of the placements were what I would of chosen and I was disappointed as I have worked in a residential home for several years and wanted to gain different experiences. I decided to see the positives and put the experience I already had in residential work to good use. Lots of my peers were initially disappointed with their first field placement, but were
>
> *continued...*

surprised at how beneficial the experiences were on completion. The more you put into your placement the more you will gain. I saw the opportunities to learn as much as I could and was able to see how this would benefit me out in the field.

To prepare for each placement, I did some research into the agency. I wanted to know the different services they provided, how they achieved them and what major legislation applied to the client base. I arranged an informal meeting with my Field Work Supervisor to discuss approaches and theories that they used and to clarify what they were expecting from me. I asked my Field Work Supervisor about relevant reading material for me to get so I could start reading up.

The two biggest challenges that I faced while on placement were trying to find evidence of my work in relation to the program learning outcomes and being seen as an extra member of staff to carry out personal support or administration duties. I did not see a social service worker at all in my first placement and only had contact with a couple in my second. I found this very frustrating as I had no previous experience of the assessment, planning and intervention process that social service workers do. I was concerned how I was going to get this experience and document it for my professional development portfolio.

To get the evidence I needed for my portfolio I had to be very proactive. I had to be persistent and make myself involved. If I saw a social worker, I would introduce myself and ask if I could sit in on their meetings and would ask if I could assist in their assessments. I found that all the social service workers that I spoke to were very understanding and this approach opened a lot of doors for me as I was invited to multi-disciplinary meetings, area offices and other community service providers to work alongside different staff. This enabled me to complete most of the requirements for my portfolio. I would also look for opportunities in the home. I would see when clients risk assessments or reviews were up coming and ask if I could complete them.

I volunteered to fill out all new client paperwork and update others.

Sometimes I found that managers on duty did not want to give me any work or were too busy to find time for me. It can be easy to lose motivation and be less enthusiastic when this happens, so I would go off and chat with the clients to get to know them and I found that by doing that I could link theories into their situations. This was beneficial to me as I learned lots just by talking to people and the clients also benefited as they really appreciated someone giving them time and just listening.

continued...

I found that the managers or staff that I worked with on placement often had differing attitudes and values. You may not agree with some opinions or they may go against the Codes of Ethics and Standards of Practice. It is important that you discuss these issues in supervision to highlight any problems or eliminate any worries you may have. I would advise students to keep a daily log as I found it hard to remember everything that I had done and being able to read through my log enabled me to recall experiences in supervision sessions. The biggest piece of advice I could give to other students about to go out on their field placement is to have confidence in yourself and not to be intimidated because of lack of experience. This is why you are on placement. It is your opportunity to learn as much as you can so be assertive and ask plenty of questions.

I am glad that I had my placements where I did as it gave me the opportunity to work with client groups that I wouldn't have otherwise experienced. I found that I gained lots of knowledge and skills that I can use in my future practice. My experiences led to job opportunities and provided me with choices for the future."

– Anonymous SSW Student

SUMMARY

Reflection on your field placement is an essential component of good practice, and not an inconvenient additional task. You are likely to find keeping a reflective journal during your placement very helpful in a variety of ways.

LEARNING OPPORTUNITIES

17

There are a variety of learning opportunities that you may be able to have during a field placement. The potential learning opportunities are detailed in the following diagram (which is not exhaustive):

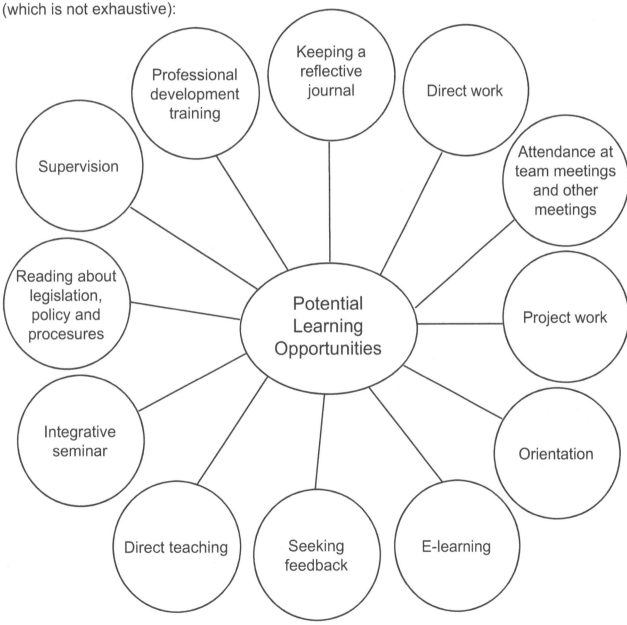

In order to learn from each opportunity, you need time to reflect and to move around the learning cycle. Simply immersing yourself in lots of activities or opportunities will not enable you to learn, even if the opportunities are good. Returning to Kolb's experiential learning cycle, you will need to:

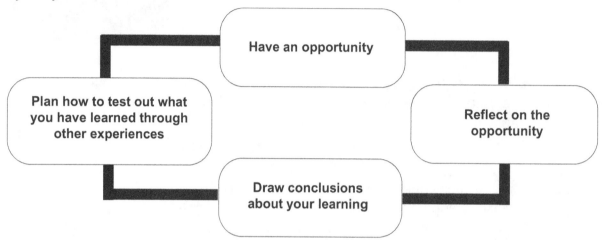

This chapter will work through some of the potential learning opportunities identified on the previous page – giving you an idea about how you can make sure you move around the full cycle following each learning experience.

Observational Visits to Other Agencies and Services

You are likely to spend some time visiting other community service providers and learn about local community resources during your orientation period. It is likely that you will find more meaningful learning in visiting a community service provider when it is particularly relevant to what you are doing in practice. For example, if you visit a community service provider when you are working with a client and want to make a referral, you are more likely to learn than if you visit during an orientation when you have nothing (or no one) to relate these experiences with.

It is important to take notes during your observational visits to community service providers. You can use the following form to record your observational visits. By detailing information about community service providers using a structured format, you will broaden your knowledge of resources available for your clients.

Student Comments on Observational Visits
Community service provider:
Date of visit:
Describe the type of setting:
Describe how referrals get made:
Strengths noted:
Weaknesses noted:
Implications of anti-oppressive issues to practice:
Future learning needs:

Reading

Field Work Supervisors and Faculty Advisors should be able to guide you towards useful reading material. This is likely to include reading relevant legislation, agency documents, policies and procedures, social work, child development, and developmental disability journals. Some of this will take place during your orientation. However, you are most likely to learn from reading material when it is specifically relevant to the work which you are doing. Therefore, it is important to prioritize what must be read early in the placement and what can be read later on, to ensure that the readings relate to what you are doing and when you are doing it.

Reading can be a passive activity, so you will need an opportunity to discuss your reading to develop your learning. You can use a range of techniques to follow up on your readings. For instance, you can take notes to discuss with your Field Work Supervisor and Faculty Advisor, develop a brief fact sheet summarizing your reading, or prepare a short presentation for a team meeting on a specific topic. Whatever you do to try to bring the reading to life, you should always make sure that you discuss your reading and its relationship to your practice in supervision and in your Integrative Seminar. This will demonstrate to your Field Work Supervisor and Faculty Advisor that you are taking an active role in your professional development and will provide you with evidence to demonstrate that you have met the program learning outcomes.

Shadowing Colleagues and Other Professionals

Students can learn a great deal from shadowing a variety of workers. After a shadowing experience, comparing and contrasting how different staff might approach similar tasks in different ways can lead to a great deal of learning and this can assist you to develop your own unique style.

However, it is important to ensure a structure is in place for the shadowing – the staff being shadowed needs to know what is expected of them and how they can help to maximize your learning, and in return you need to know what specifically you are hoping to gain from the experience.

Le Riche (2006) describes the importance of observing the practice of others and states that:

> Observation can play a significant part in enabling (you) to become increasingly aware of the significance of power relations and anti-oppressive practice in working with service users.

By taking on the role of an observer, you can more accurately imagine and empathize with the experience of a client through witnessing the contact between the client and the worker who you are shadowing. Through observation, this can enable you to pick out the language, ideas, communication strategies and techniques which you can then adapt into your own future practice, as well as discarding any ideas which you find do not fit with your own style and perception of what works. Thoughtfully, considering shadowing observations should enable you to be clearer in your reflections as to what you feel your own working style will look like. In brief, this is what the "use of self" means – this is a concept many social service workers and other human service workers are familiar with. Consider, how do you "use" yourself to engage with clients in terms of your:

- Speech: cadence, tone
- Language: choice of words and phrases
- Body language
- Eye contact
- Posture
- Use of humour (where appropriate)
- Facial expressions
- Ability to challenge or provide feedback

The list could go on indefinitely.

The following guidance on offering shadowing experience (which is given to the worker being shadowed) and shadowing form (completed by you and the worker you have shadowed) may be useful in making the most of shadowing opportunities. This form has been tailored to a SSW field placement; however, this could be altered for field placements in DSW, CYW or other related human service programs of study.

GUIDANCE ON OFFERING SHADOWING EXPERIENCE

Thank you for offering a social service worker student the opportunity to shadow your practice. As you know, learning from effective role models is very useful and an essential part of social service work field placement learning.

"Shadowing" can mean different things to different people. Demonstrating competence as a social service worker student is the responsibility of the student in consultation with their Field Work Supervisor. However, there are some implications for you, having offered your service to provide this shadowing opportunity.

You will need to explain the context of the work to the student who is to shadow you. This will enable them to maximize their learning from the experience. The student should feel able to ask you some questions to clarify any points.

During their field placement experience social service work students are expected to demonstrate that they can work effectively within the scope of practice of a social service worker while meeting the program learning outcomes for their field of study. This has been broken down into nine program learning outcomes:

1. Develop and maintain professional relationships which adhere to professional, legal, and ethical standards aligned to social service work.

2. Identify strengths, resources, and challenges of individuals, families, groups, and communities to assist them in achieving their goals.

3. Recognize diverse needs and experiences of individuals, groups, families, and communities to promote accessible and responsive programs and services.

4. Identify current social policy, relevant legislation, and political, social, and economic systems and their impacts on service delivery.

5. Advocate for appropriate access to resources to assist individuals, families, groups, and communities.

6. Develop and maintain positive working relationships with colleagues, supervisors, and community partners.

7. Develop strategies and plans that lead to the promotion of self-care, improved job performance, and enhanced work relationships.

8. Integrate social group work and group facilitation skills across a wide range of environments, supporting growth and development of individuals, families, and communities.

continued...

---

9. Work in communities to advocate for change strategies that promote social and economic justice and challenge patterns of oppression and discrimination.

It would be helpful if you could enable the student to consider as many of these areas as possible when they are shadowing you. For example if they have observed you demonstrating program learning outcomes 1, 2, 3, 4 and 5. If you could discuss how these outcomes are put into practice, this would be very helpful.

The student will be asked to complete a short form about their experience of shadowing and what they have learned. There is space on this for you to make any comments. For example, you may have observed the student communicating with the client and others, you may have discussed relevant organizational policies with the student and they may have demonstrated they have a good level of understanding. All of this feedback will be helpful to the Field Work Supervisor when they are gathering information for the final evaluation of the student's performance on field placement.

These questions could be spread across a few pages to give you both opportunities to record all of your comments in relation to the shadowing experience. While the Guidance for Shadowing Experience and the Shadow report have been tailored to SSW program outcomes, similar documents could be created for other programs of study.

SHADOWING REPORT

Student's name:

Name of worker shadowed:

Date of shadowing:

STUDENT TO COMPLETE

What did you shadow?

What did you learn from the experience?

What questions do you have as a result of the experience?

Which of the social service worker program learning outcomes did you see in action during the shadowing?

What would you like to gain from future shadowing opportunities?

WORKER SHADOWED TO COMPLETE

Comments about the student / shadowing experience

Student:	Signature & Date:
Worker Shadowed:	Signature & Date:
Field Work Supervisor:	Signature & Date:

Professional Development Training:

Many agencies, organizations and institutions have a variety of in-house training opportunities that may be offered to you as part of your field placement.

With limited professional development budgets for staff, most agencies, organizations and institutions prioritize employees rather than students for training opportunities, which in many ways is understandable. You may be told that you can't attend a course because there is limited space or resources available. Despite the limited resources and budget restraints, a number of agencies, organization and institutions have supported students in attending staff training in-house as well as off-site in the community.

> "Don't be afraid to ask for things such as opportunities to shadow other professionals visiting other agencies, getting involved in team days, and accessing training. Actually the training one is a good one – some people think students don't need to be on other training during placements, but I always think you get as much (if not more) from the people on the course as you do from the course itself, so training is a good opportunity to learn from more experienced professionals."
>
> *– (SWAP, 2007)*

Project Work

Students can learn a great deal from project work, and the staff within an agency, organization or institution often benefit when a student takes a special project – this is typically a "win-win" situation for all parties involved. Essentially, a project should not be an academic piece of work – this is field placement after all – but outside of this, the range of projects is potentially immense. Examples of some of the projects students have worked on throughout field placements include:

- the development of a community resource binder for the staff
- creating a educational group proposal
- development of information packages for clients
- evaluation of outcomes for clients
- developing project plans for specific areas of work with clients
- developing strategies for work with clients whose first language isn't English.

As a starting point to develop ideas for project work, talk with the staff and your Field Work Supervisor about what they would really like to do if they had the time. You could then follow this up with the question: "If I were to undertake this piece of work, would it assist my learning and help me in providing the evidence I need to meet the program learning outcomes for my program of study?" If the answer to this is yes, then the potential project could offer you an incredible learning experience.

Remember, you are only with the agency, organization or institution for a limited amount of time so any project should be clearly defined and manageable within the appropriate time-frames.

E-learning

E-learning refers to the use of information and communication technologies such as computer based learning programs and use of the Internet to assist learning. E-learning is widely promoted in all work environments including the college where you are taking your program of study.

Some colleges set up e-learning courses which students continue taking during field place-ment (some colleges offer the Integrative Field Placement Seminar online). Some colleges are also developing the use of electronic evaluations which Field Work Supervisors can complete online to save paperwork. Some agencies, organizations and institution also have e-learning courses which students can access to assist their learning and orientation to the practicum site.

The Association of Social Work Board (ASWB) has a fairly well developed e-learning continuing education course database – information can be accessed on their website – www.aswb.org/education/providers. The social policy and social work subject centre of the Higher Education Academy (known as SWAP) connects people to a range of e-learning resources for field placement, via their website – www.swap.ac.uk.

A large number of agencies, organizations and institutions subscribe to a number of social work journals and enable Field Work Supervisors, staff and field placement students to have access through their subscription.

Reflective Journals

See Chapter 16 for advice on how to make the most of the learning opportunities which reflective journals can provide.

Direct Work

You should be given the opportunity to engage in a range of direct practice with clients, groups and communities depending on the field placement setting. This might include case work, group work, advocacy and community work. You will also participate in staff meetings and other activities. However, while you do need the opportunity to engage in "real work," it is vital that you are not seen as an extra worker who can be overloaded with work. One of the purposes of having a Field Work Supervisor is to assign workload and this needs to be made clear with staff at the beginning of the field placement. Generally, all of the work you are asked to do should be assigned through your Field Work Supervisor or supervisor (where relevant). It is not uncommon for staff members, in their enthusiasm to provide useful opportunities to overload a student, particularly as you may find it difficult to feel able to say no. Remember not everyone will know what you have on your plate and staff members might offer you lots of opportunities which you are keen to take on, but it is important not to overload yourself.

Direct Teaching

A didactic approach to teaching is basically about telling people how to do things. There will be a few instances during a placement where a Field Work Supervisor or supervisor may need to take this approach, for example, in informing you about specific processes. However, it is important to remember that your Field Work Supervisor's main role is that of a facilitator and not a teacher (Williams & Rutter, 2007):

> Practice educators will not always be 'experts' in their field and more traditional didactic / transmission method of teaching…will not be the most appropriate way for developing professional capability, as well as not being the most appropriate approach for work based learning.

Your Field Work Supervisor will expect you to take some initiative in being self directed. For instance, in preparing for your supervision session, you may be required to do research into a specific topic or theory. Or you could be required to research best practices on techniques and methods of interventions. Your Field Work Supervisor is not being lazy or dodging their responsibility – they are promoting the best way for you to learn.

Supervision Exercises and Discussion

Many of the learning opportunities covered in this chapter come together in supervision, and the follow up discussions about your learning opportunities which will take place during your supervision is important. Your Field Work Supervisor might suggest specific exercises for you as a tool for discussion to develop your learning during supervision. General supervision discussion in itself can be a major learning opportunity for many students.

Supervision is such an important aspect of field placement that Section E is dedicated fully to it.

SUMMARY

There are a number of potential learning opportunities that will be available to you during your placement. Opportunities should be selected based on your individual goals and objectives and which match your preferred learning style. It is essential that learning opportunities balance the specific learning requirements for your program of study with what is manageable in terms of workload. More importantly, students need to be proactive about their learning, seeking out learning opportunities and making the most of them.

"Getting the most out of a placement is all about how much you put into it. In my opinion, placement experiences are not only an opportunity to achieve the necessary outcomes for the diploma, but also a chance to 'taste' the various sectors, whether you are in government mandated, commercial or the voluntary sector. Field Placement provides you with the potential for networking and as a means of gaining a positive reputation within the community, this is crucial when requesting references for future job opportunities.

Your reputation as a developmental service worker depends upon your ability to communicate effectively with clients, team members and other professionals. As a student, you may find yourself in a position where you may wish to challenge others practice, as in my situation. I would advise you to utilize the supervision and support available to students to discuss and explore strategies in which to address any contentious issues, as I think it is important to adopt a sensitive approach to any challenges you may wish to raise, in order to maintain positive working relationships.

I was particularly lucky with the placements I was offered through my college. I gained from experience within both adults and children's, within both the commercial and voluntary sectors. However, there were occasions when I felt that the placement may not provide opportunities to fulfill the necessary criteria. I found it helpful to liaise with other staff and agencies that linked with the organization that I was placed within. This enabled me to create projects or tasks in order to complete the required elements of performance for my professional development portfolio. Again, this opportunity provided further networking opportunities in addition to a wider understanding of the roles of other professionals and resulted in me becoming a committee member of the organization that I had undertaken some work with."

– Anonymous DSW Student

BALANCING YOUR LEARNING WITH OTHER REQUIREMENTS OF THE FIELD PLACEMENT

18

Many social service work students look forward to their placement as the time when they will be able to do actual social service work. Sometimes students cannot see the how their course work prepares them for their professional practice. People who typically choose to do vocational training in such areas as Social Service Worker, Developmental Service Worker, Child and Youth Worker and other human services related work are usually people who have a keen will to assist others and who enjoy working and learning.

When you are on placement, it is important to remember that a lot of what you will be asked to do is consider how **you** can make that connections between your learning in class to your role in the field. Your role on field placement can seem divided between doing the job and being a student as the following table shows:

Time "doing the job"	Time "being a student"
• Home visits	• Job shadowing (throughout your placement)
• Individual planned work with clients	• Networking / agency observational visits
• Writing up assessments and plans	• Reflecting / doing your reflective journal
• Co-ordinating services and supports	• Supervision (and planning for this)
• Staff meetings	• Field Integration Seminars (and planning for this)

Many students can feel that the tasks in the right hand column have less importance than those on the left because placements are all about learning from doing the job. However, the difference between you and your colleagues in the practicum site is that you are the one who is being evaluated. You need to permit yourself to take the time to do these tasks to prepare you for your final evaluation. Learning to balance your learning within your field placement will prepare you for your future career.

We know that allowing time for learning can sometimes feel frustrating, particularly for students who have worked in the field for some time, but it is vital that you do take on the student role and maintain an appropriate balance as your final evaluation will depend on this. Being the student is beneficial because you are able to take the time to reflect, to read, to learn and to share this learning with others in the agency, organization or institution.

Time Management

Effective time management is a key skill for all students as the role can be so high pressured, varied and sometimes stressful. Managing your time on placement effectively is critical. By managing the competing demands of a placement you are demonstrating that you are likely to be able to manage a complex and busy workload out in the field.

Time management is a skill that many of us have to learn. It is essential to being effective in the human service sectors, as many workers have different competing demands (for example, direct work with clients, documentation, and or advocating for community resources) which they find the most rewarding, challenging and satisfying. For example, a social service worker who has done the psychosocial report with a child, but not the occurrence report for the court hearing that is due tomorrow will not be judged as effective. Similarly, the most empathetic and considerate social service worker working in Adult Protective Service, who has done a thorough assessment and engaged with the client with respect and dignity, will not be viewed in such a positive light by the family when the deadline date has been missed because they did not have enough time to compile the necessary documentation and recommendations.

There are some fairly common time management problems and not dealing with these can restrict the amount of time which you have and make you feel like you are drowning at work. These can include:

- Procrastination-putting things off
- Difficulty prioritizing the tasks
- Inadequate personal organization
- Setting unrealistic goals or objectives

> "Effective time management will mean you can retain a life and not be a victim of your work."
>
> – (SWAP, 2007)

The latter is an issue which you may choose to address in supervision and it is a useful exercise to have a checkpoint with your Field Work Supervisor each time you have supervision, as this can ensure that your deadline and timeframes line up. You may notice that having too much to do does not appear on this list. While it may be true that there is a great deal to do when you are on placement, the way that people manage themselves and their time can almost always be improved.

How to Manage Your Time

- Be effective in your daily planning
- Use "to do" lists
- Prioritize effectively
- Break down large tasks into smaller more achievable tasks
- Work on your decision making skills. Don't procrastinate
- Manage your environment effectively
- Don't let workload tasks dominate over tasks which you need to do as part of your learning (or vise versa)
- Manage phone calls and emails effectively
- Keep a set time to prepare for supervision

This might look like a big list of things to do, but an effective social service worker will incorporate most of these time management strategies into their daily practice. Too often other professionals complain about workers who never return their phone calls. Time management can often depend on a good "to do" list where the tasks for the day or week are broken down into chunks which are achievable within the time you have available between meetings or appointments.

Managing your environment may sound insignificant, but knowing where to find the tools you need quickly can be important. Busy people often have messy desks but when a messy desk interferes with one's ability to be effective and efficient, this can be problematic. Responding to emails can be time consuming; deleting or filing ones you do not need can be a great way of making sure you feel on top of your in-box.

The Environment

- Keep your desk clear
- Use systems such as in trays and out trays
- If possible check emails at set times – don't set an alert to tell you every time you have a new email, unless you are awaiting an urgent one!
- Make sure you use any available voice mail or redirect calls when necessary
- Manage paper: the idea is that you should only need to touch each piece of paper once, then file, action or recycle it!

To Do Lists

- Each task should take no more than one to two hours (break down larger tasks)
- Indicate what is urgent and what is important (these are not necessarily the same!) using a coding system if it helps
- Keep the list up-to-date
- You might want to keep more than one list (e.g., an overview list and a daily list) but don't just end up with lots of lists
- If you find yourself writing a new to do list (say each week or month) and the same thing keeps getting put on the list and never seems to be achieved, think about whether the task needs doing at all (or why you may be avoiding it!)

Daily Planning

- Allocate time for important tasks
- Allocate time for "unknowns" – you might not know what the time will be used for, but if you plan the time, other important things won't get pushed out when something arises. If nothing comes up you can use the time to get through other things on your to do list
- Don't forget the basics (e.g., allowing travel time where necessary)

In order to achieve the things you must do as part of your placement, you need to be able to prioritize tasks. In selecting priorities, it is essential to differentiate between "important" and "urgent." "Important" suggests value so a task could be important in terms of the outcome of your placement or the effectiveness of the service for one of your clients, but some important tasks can only be completed towards the end of your time on placement. "Urgent" refers to tasks which need to be done now. It might be helpful to plot your range of tasks as illustrated in the following table.

	Very Important	Quite Important	Not Important
Very urgent	Complete assessment for Case Management Team Meeting tomorrow	Return call from school C	Clear emails
Quite urgent	Complete reading for supervision on Thursday, and compile evidence for program learning outcomes	Arrange to visit client who has recently been assigned	Arrange shadowing with agency
Not urgent	Complete portfolio	Do background research for planned work with family F	

If you like working with numbers, you can give tasks a score – 3 points for very important or very urgent, 2 for quite important or urgent, and 1 for not important or urgent. Then multiply one number by another so something in the very important and very urgent box would be 3X3 = 9. Task which may end up in the shaded box clearly represent items that can be avoided till all other tasks have been performed! The same does not apply though for items in the "not urgent" row as these are the tasks you need to plan for well in advance. These tasks have a habit of reaching the very urgent box before you have considered when you will have time to fit them in!

> **“**Just look at what you have to do this week. Break everything down into small tasks. If you look at the enormity of what you have to do it will blow your mind and you'll be discouraged before you start.**”**
>
> *– (SWAP, 2007)*

SUMMARY

Being a social service work student on placement involves balancing your role and your competing demands. Developing solid time management skills can help you achieve this balance.

KEY LEARNING POINTS: SECTION D

- It is important to agree on the Learning Contract for your field placement by working in partnership with your Field Work Supervisor

- Students should be fully engaged in the learning process and should take responsibility for their own learning

- Learning is a two way process – you should take every opportunity to learn as much from your role as possible

- It is helpful to have at least a basic understanding of adult learning theory to make sure that you get the most from your learning in your placement

- Reflecting on your learning is essential. Keeping a reflective journal can be very helpful with this

- A wide range of learning opportunities are available within any field placement setting

- The role of a Field Work Supervisor is about facilitating your learning rather than directly teaching

- Developing your skills around effective time management can help you to meet the challenging demands around balancing learning with assigned work load

- You get out of field placement what you put into it!

HOW TO MAKE EFFECTIVE USE OF SUPERVISION

Supervision sessions should allow you to consolidate your learning and strengthen your capacity to self assess your skills and abilities. As such supervision is an essential part of your field placement. Supervision is a two way process requiring work on the part of the students and the Field Work Supervisor.

This section explores how to make effective use of the supervision process during your placement in order to get the most from it.

SUPERVISION STYLES

19

"When I consider issues around learning within a placement, I cannot help but link this directly with the use of supervision. Supervision was my opportunity to discuss, explore, challenge and evaluate the information that I was processing while learning on placement. It provided me with the opportunity to 'bounce' ideas within a safe environment. I have been fortunate within the three placements that I have taken. I gained from the knowledge and experience that my supervisors and mentors bought to the supervision sessions. They provided the milieu for me to speak openly and honestly about my own values and how they impact upon my practice. The ability to form a positive working relationship with your supervisor or mentor will heighten the potential to gain personally and professionally from the placement.

I found it particularly helpful when my supervisor suggested a task to discover the learning styles that best suited my individual personality. This exercise enabled me to consider how I learn, what is helpful and what is unhelpful. From this I gauged that I like time to research and prepare before undertaking tasks. My supervisor used this information by pre-setting particular learning tasks in advance of supervision sessions, for example, to research a particular theory or model of practice and relate it to my experiences on placement. This may be a useful tool for other students to gain the maximum benefit from supervision sessions.

My other tip, is preparation! I believe that that students will get out what they put in from their placement – it is up to you! In a very busy team, the luxury of in-depth, 'time-protected' supervision, in my opinion, is not to be wasted."

– Anonymous CYW Student

What is supervision?

The word "supervision" can sound confusing to many students, particularly if you have not had any prior experience of professional supervision in the field. For some students, the term supervision conjures up a visual image of someone overseeing all aspects of your work directly. However, in a professional context, supervision isn't about someone watching you all the time.

"Social Work in general has been defined as a supervising profession" (Kadushin & Harkness, 2002). "Social Work practice was built on the foundation of supervision" (Harkness & Poertner, 1989) and continues to be a central component to ethical social service worker practice. The research suggests that good quality supervision leads to enhanced job retention, increased job satisfaction, reduced turnover and protects practitioners against burnout in the field of social work (Bogo, Patterson, Tufford, & King, 2011). More importantly, supervision promotes high quality care for clients and is a requirement for both Social Workers and Social Service Worker under the College's Standards of Practice (OCSWSSW, 2012).

According to Kadushin (1985), professional supervision in social work and social welfare has three functions:

1. Educative

- supports the development of skills and knowledge
- promotes reflective practice
- leads to professional competence

2. Administrative

- ensures adherence to the Codes of Ethics and Standards of Practice, relevant legislation and agency policies
- monitors and evaluates work performance

1. Supportive

- builds and maintains working relationships, morale and job satisfaction

Morrison (2005) expanded on the model and provides a clear definition of supervision with four commonly agreed upon functions of supervision.

1. *Managerial/Normative Function*: focuses on addressing the administrative tasks of assigning and managing work loads.

2. *Developmental/Formative Function*: focuses on learning and professional growth.

3. ***Supportive/Restorative function***: focuses on personal support targeted at reducing anxiety.

4. ***Mediation Function***: focuses on negotiation/engaging the individual with the organization.

Supervision in the field often will focus on the managerial function more than the other forms of supervision. It is essential that in your supervision as a student, all four functions are covered – with perhaps the primary focus being on the developmental function around your learning. So, while Morrison's framework has been developed for practitioners in the field, this model has been adapted for field placement supervision. For example (Australiian Learning & Teaching Council, 2010):

1. Administration/Management: learning about the workplace

2. Education: doing, thinking and reflecting

3. Support: thriving

4. Mediating: negotiating and advocating in the system and in relationships

5. Socialization: becoming and being apart of the profession

Administrative/Management

As a student you need to be given the opportunity to discuss your workload, the reasons for caseload assignments, and the work you are carrying out, planned or expected outcomes, challenges and concerns. All of these discussions are part of the administrative and accountability aspect of supervision described by Morrison (2005) as the managerial or normative function.

Education

What Morrison (2005) refers to as the developmental or formative function, others referred to it as the educative function (Kadushin, 1985).

When you discuss the work that you have been doing, you should also take the opportunity to reflect on what you learned from each experience. Supervision should be a key element in your learning experience, bringing together experiences which allow you space and time to discuss your thoughts, feelings, reflections, observations, concerns, difficulties and how you have or may address these elements. Bogo and Vayda (1998) developed a four-step Integration of Theory and Practice (ITP) Loop that is useful in facilitating this educative process.

Retrieval
- Obtain information regarding the field placement situation

Reflection
- Reflect on retrieved information and examine your personal associations and feelings regarding the information presented to you by the client, which then leads to an objective and sensitive assessment.

Linkage
- Identify and utilize your knowledge to explain both the retrieved information and your reflection on the information.
- This is where the student makes a conscious application of theory to practice.

Professional Response
- Analyze the information to formulate a professional response from which a plan is developed.

Support

Supervision should be a supportive process. Work in this field can evoke a variety of emotions and reactions and you are likely to need support with this. On placement, you might feel that you are being asked to deal with experiences such as poverty and scarcity, which you might find upsetting. Coupled with this, you are managing your workload and your learning with the requirements of the Field Integration Seminar. In addition, many students work part time to support themselves financially. It is no surprise that field placements can be a very stressful experience for many students. Field Work Supervisors and Faculty Advisors are well aware of this.

The four steps identified in the Integration of Theory and Practice Loop is useful to being able to process and structure the support needed during field placement. However, it is important to acknowledge boundaries here – a supervision session should not become a counselling session. Supportive supervision is important, but this should not be at the expense of the other functions of supervision. If you need support over and above what can be offered within a well-balanced supervision session, a Field Work Supervisor can advise you about other resources available. Most colleges have counselling services, and some agencies have similar supports in place and it may be appropriate for you to consider accessing these if needed.

While it is important that a Field Work Supervisor is supportive, there must be a balance – your Field Work Supervisor is your supervisor not your counsellor, and this is a learning relationship. It is critical to maintain healthy boundaries.

Mediation

This function of supervision is less commonly written about, yet it is an important aspect of supervision. Mediation is a key aspect of all professional supervision, including your supervision on field placement. Morrison (2005) asserts that the mediation function of supervision is about a supervisor:

- negotiating and clarifying staff roles and responsibilities
- consulting with management about resources and the implications of lack of resources
- allocating resources in the most efficient and effective way
- representing the needs of staff and advocating when needed
- consulting and updating staff about organizational developments or information
- mediating or advocating between workers, within teams, within other parts of the agency, organization or institution or with outside agencies including community partners

Sometimes, you may feel discouraged about what can be achieved with some clients. A Field Work Supervisor may use supervision to explore your feelings and understanding of key issues about service provision, empowerment, and what people need to do for themselves. A number of studies (Maclean, 2007) indicate that students are poorly prepared for the current climate of resource scarcity. The mediation function can help you to understand the bigger picture. Resource issues including funding allocations, eligibility for services, and appropriate strategies for advocating on behalf of clients are all important components of the mediation function.

> **“**Try to find a balance between idealism and realism that may help you to remain motivated and enthusiastic when faced with boundaries and limitations in practice.**”**
>
> – (SWAP, 2007)

Socialization

Socialization refers to the learning of social roles, the processes through which a student develops a professional self. The development of a professional self includes adopting the values, attitudes, knowledge, and skills, fusing these into a set of characteristics which are accepted by professionals in the field. Field Work Supervisors and Faculty Advisors support students in the socialization process. Becoming a social service worker involves the integration of professional and personal identity using various formal and informal socialization experiences that comprise social service work education (Webb, 1988).

When considering the importance of the supervisory role in the formal education process, Kadushin (1992) identified "the objective of professional training is...to socialize the student to the ways of the profession, to develop a professional conscience...the elaborate process of professional socialization" (Kadushin, 1992).

The five main functions of supervision balance the needs of all parties involved in a practicum site. In short, the supervisory relationship between the Field Work Supervisor and student assumes a prominent role in the transmission, assimilation and application of the values, knowledge and skills required of the profession. Having a clear framework for your supervision as a student is important so that everyone is clear about its purpose. The following guidelines facilitate the discussion between you and your Field Work Supervisor, and it can form the basis of a supervision agreement.

A Framework For Student Supervision on Field Placement

Field work supervision is one of the most important aspects of the students learning experience, it provides the framework for students to examine their practice, to grow, and develop personally and professionally. Given that each field placement setting and each student may require a different style of supervision, most Social Service Worker programs are aware that some flexibility is necessary. Yet at the same time, uniform standards need to be established to ensure a quality learning experience for students on field placement. The following guidelines have therefore been established:

- Supervision should facilitate a student's learning, professional and personal development. The supervision should tie to the program outcomes and reflect the scope of practice of the student for the intended designation. (Refer to Chapter 1.)

- The primary focus for all supervision should address the learning objectives and skill development outcomes of the students. Supervision should be planned, reflective and provide students with an opportunity to link theory to practice. (Refer to ITP Loop.)

- Each student requires a minimum of 1-1.5 hours per week of regularly scheduled supervision meetings. Frequency and duration should be agreed at the beginning of the field placement.

- Supervision sessions should include regular feedback on the student's performance, including both the strengths and the areas requiring further development as it pertains to the program learning outcomes. Field Work Supervisor's expectations need to be clear and concise to ensure that the student has reasonable opportunity to modify or change their behaviours accordingly.

- Supervision should focus upon the student's use of self within practice and aligned to the Code of Ethics and Standards of Practice outlined by the professional body regulating their profession, to boundaries, to expectations and policies of the agency, organization or institution.

- Supervision sessions should address the imbalance of power between the Field Work Supervisor and student relationship and the complexity of power relationships in the workplace more generally.

- Conflict resolution should take place, in the first instance, within the supervision process. If issues remain unresolved, identified procedures should be followed without delay with the Faculty Advisor.

Model of Supervision

Davys & Biddoe (2000) developed a Field Supervision Model that build on Kolb's Experiential Learning Cycle (Kolb, 1984) and is an adaptation of the work of Ford & Jones (1987). The Field Supervision Model includes a Beginning, Agenda Setting, a Supervision Cycle and an Ending.

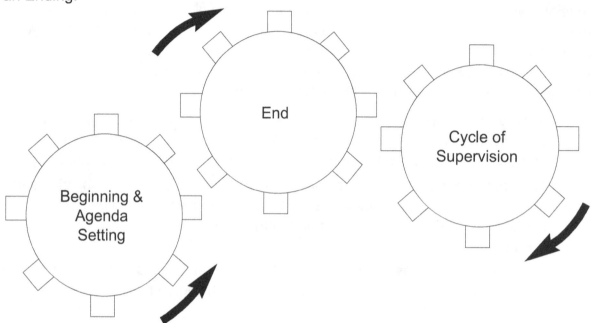

Beginning & Agenda Setting

Quality supervision requires focus, energy, commitment and trust between the Field Work Supervisor and the student. Trust and respect begins to form at the start of the placement when expectation and responsibilities are identified and negotiated between Field Work Supervisor and student. Supervision sessions build on trust. Sessions typically begin with each party being invited to begin with themselves and then making the transition to collect and focus their thoughts on the supervision session.

Setting the agenda for supervision is usually done by the student. Initially, the agendas should be jointly constructed, with the previously stated aims in mind. Standing items (such as anti-oppressive practice and theory to practice) can be useful to ensure aims are achieved. When supervision is regularly scheduled, it allows for both you and your Field Work Supervisor to plan and prepare for the session. So, while the primary responsibility of the agenda may be with the student, the Field Work Supervisors will need to take responsibility for ensuring that critical issues such as: students ambivalence about autonomy, matters of competence, ethics, emotional awareness, power and control, cultural awareness, risk management and personal care are placed on the agenda for supervision.

Cycle of Supervision

The cycle of supervision includes a progression of stages, the reality is that presenting a process in a linear way is not very realistic yet is useful to conceptualize for our understanding of flow. The Field Supervision Model presents the cycle of supervision from the beginning, agenda setting and the ending. This is to represent the fact that the cycle repeats itself for each separate issue or problem identified in a supervision session, and it is not until the conclusion of the session that a final ending will be made. Within the cycle of supervision the following stages have been identified:

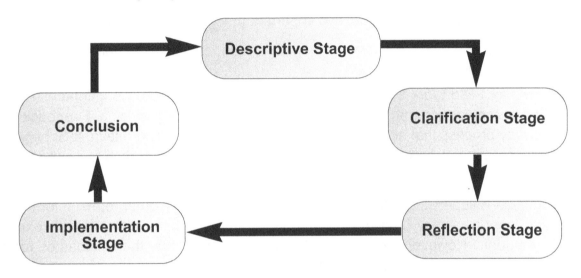

Descriptive Stage: after prioritizing the agenda, the first step of supervision typically begins with you revisiting an experience on field placement. You need to be able to do this with minimal interruption as the intent is for you to gain an awareness of the experience through the task of retelling.

Clarification Stage: allows the Field Work Supervisor to establish a clear understanding of the situation. Essentially, there are two goals: identify the problem brought forward objectively and to consider why you chose this particular problem to bring forward.

Reflection Stage: provides time, space, and support for you to learn the process of critical reflection in relation to your practice. Consider the following questions:

- What feeling are you most aware and how did these get expressed? What did you intuitively do? What were your thoughts or judgements during and after? What did you learn about yourself when thinking about your response to the situation? What would you like to do if faced with a similar situation? What impact has structural restraints had on the situation?

Implementation Stage: allows you and your Field Work Supervisor to develop a plan of action. Field Work Supervisors may consider the following strategies:

- Formal teaching, planning and role-playing situations, assessing and developing clinical practice skills, integration of theory into practice, exploring potential learning opportunities as an ongoing process, reviewing learning goals and objectives in the learning contract, identifying optimum learning and teaching styles, and identifying personal support required.

Endings

The end of a supervision session has two important functions:

- It summarize the significant learning experiences, conclusions, decisions and future tasks as a result of the session.

- Allows for Field Work Supervisor to provide feedback on your work done in the supervision session and to comment on the process of supervision. Feedback is a two-way process that needs to be constructive, balanced and relevant. Supervision, as a process, will be continually evaluated and open to adaptation to meet challenging needs.

Formal structured supervision sessions can be complimented by other forms: informal supervision, peer supervision and group supervision. All of which can be valuable experiences for students. However, these should be in addition to, rather than instead of, formal two-way sessions between Field Work Supervisors and students.

Supervision arrangements may be incorporated in the Learning Contract. A separate supervision agreement can be drawn up. This ensures that both student and Field Work Supervisors are aware of the expectations for supervision. The boundaries of confidentiality within supervision should be explicitly agreed between the Field Work Supervisor and student at this time.

What to Expect From Supervision as a Student

Some students will be used to supervision from their previous course work experiences. It is important to be aware that student supervision and employee supervision differs in a number of ways.

- *Regularity*: your supervision as a student should be much more regular than that of workers.

- *Variety of approaches*: a variety of approaches are likely to be used in student supervision – for example, role playing and case studies. Anything which will facilitate your learning may be used in your supervision. While there may be some variety in supervision with employees, on the whole it will focus on discussion about cases.

- *Theory and other underpinning knowledge*: while your supervision sessions as a student will include discussion about social work theory and other underpinning knowledge, unfortunately, this is often less obvious within professional supervision.

- *Emphasis*: the emphasis in student supervision is on learning and reflection. While it could be argued that there should be a similar emphasis in professional supervision, this is often not the case. The focus of professional supervision is often on accountability for workload.

- *Learning goals*: your learning goals and objective should be addressed within the supervision process. In fact, the main purpose of student supervision is to address your learning needs and ensure that your placement is running smoothly.

- *Assessment*: while student supervision is all about your learning, it is also a forum used for evaluating your skills and abilities in relation to program learning outcomes. Most professional supervision does not include an assessment element (at least not formally).

- *Direct involvement*: The person providing supervision to you (i.e., the Field Work Supervisor and where relevant, on-site supervisor) will have some direct knowledge of the work which you are doing. They may be co-working cases for example. As a minimum, there will have been a number of direct observations of your work. For workers, often the person providing professional supervision has little or no direct knowledge of the work being undertaken such that they are reliant on the worker's reports about the work.

- *Evidence of work*: since it is likely that the records of your supervision will be used as part of the evaluation process, often being included in your professional development portfolio, the recording of student supervision is often different to that of workers.

- *Length of process / relationship*: student supervision relationships are by their very nature short term. When the placement ends, the supervision process and the supervisory relationship also ends. On the other hand, professional supervisory processes and relationships are open-ended and usually continue on a long term basis until either the supervisor or supervisee moves positions.

- *Gains / Outcomes*: It could be argued that because of the assessment component, there is more of an obvious outcome or personal gain for you as a student than for a worker in supervision.

Perhaps because of the significant differences between the supervision of students and the supervision of workers, there is a long standing debate about whether the word "supervision" for what occurs with students, should be used. Shardlow and Doel (1996) use the term practice tutorial rather than supervision. It is both appropriate and useful to use the word supervision simply because it what is used within the field.

Supervision Agreements

It is important to have a clear agreement about supervision covering issues such as regularity, venue, agenda, duration, boundaries and responsibilities. Some Field Work Supervisors devote a section of the Learning Contract to this; others devise a separate supervision agreement. This document should be signed by you and your Field Work Supervisor. Try to make sure that you negotiate the following areas with your Field Work Supervisor:

- What is expected of you in terms of preparation for each session
- When and where supervision sessions will take place
- Who will record supervision discussions and in what detail (see Chapter 21)
- How actions agreed within supervision will be monitored and reviewed
- What the boundaries of confidentiality will be regarding your supervision discussions
- How tasks set for supervision sessions will meet your identified learning goals and objectives and your preferred learning style(s)
- Whether supervision can be interrupted, by whom, and in which exceptional circumstances
- Practical issues such as what to do about cell phones, refreshments, length of sessions and breaks
- What to do if you disagree about any issues and who you may approach to help resolve conflicts

By formalizing the field placement supervision it becomes: (1) a planned contact between you and your Field Work Supervisor, (2) which both of you have prepared for, (3) for the purpose of discussing professional issues, (4) planning subsequent interventions or projects, and (5) and is used to generate feedback (Alle-Corliss & Alle-Corliss, 1999; Chiaferri & Griffin, 1997; Thomlinson, Rogers, Collins, & Ginnell, 1996; Wilson, 1981).

Frequency and Duration

You should have regular formal supervision sessions with your Field Work Supervisor. Most programs have their own requirements on frequency and duration – check out your program handbook as this is likely to clarify your requirements. Most programs require 1-1.5 hours per week. If you are a part time student, this would be provided on a pro-rated basis. In addition to these formal sessions, you should be able to access informal consultation at other times (in the case of offsite Supervisors, this informal consultation will be provided by the onsite supervisor).

Location and Other Practical Arrangements

Supervision should always take place in a private location where there will be no interruptions. Part of a supervision agreement might identify a suitable room for supervision. The actual environment is not that important – it is rare for field placement environments to have beautifully decorated rooms with plush comfortable furniture. It is, however, worth considering some of the practical issues of the environment, as this can be so intrinsically linked to power and how comfortable you find supervision sessions. For example, if there is a desk or table, can you both sit on the same side? If there are only two chairs and one is substantially higher or bigger than the other, who should take this one? etc. Don't forget some of the basics too – like switching off phones in the room and putting a note on the door to avoid any interruptions. Often Field Work Supervisors ask students to take responsibility for booking the room for supervision. Make sure you are clear about how to do this and that you do make the bookings!

Supervision Agendas

Every supervision session should have an agenda. Some Field Work Supervisors agree a standing agenda for all supervision sessions; some set an agenda for supervision at the end of the previous session. Other Field Work Supervisors ask the student to set the agenda. Whatever process is used, you should be given the opportunity to revisit the agenda and add to it at the start of each session. Your Field Work Supervisors will expect to see you take initiative in setting the agenda. It is important to make a note of anything you want to raise in supervision and that you take these notes to each supervision session adding to the agenda as the session begins.

> **Top Tips for Getting the Most out of Supervision**
>
> - Make sure you play an active part in negotiating the supervision agreement
> - Clarify your responsibilities with respect to supervision and meeting them
> - Be proactive in agenda setting
> - Give supervision the priority it deserves
> - Prepare effectively for every session

How to Prepare for Supervision

Preparing for supervision is important as the contact can otherwise turn from one which you look forward to and is beneficial to your learning into two or three hours of anxiety! Preparation for the next supervision can begin the moment your last supervision ends. Your supervision notes should be checked by both you and your Field Work Supervisors and actions which have been agreed should be planned into your journal so that you have time to achieve everything which has been asked of you.

Effective preparation might also include:

- Checking your learning contract and spending some time doing background reading on key topics before they reach your supervision agenda
- Reflecting on your experiences since the last session and making notes about what you want to add to the agenda or anything you want to raise

- Gathering evidence of your program learning outcomes for your professional development portfolio and having them ready for supervision sessions

- Specific tasks set by your Field Work Supervisors and agreed by you

- Re-reading your supervision notes the day before your session and checking that you have completed all actions detailed

- Checking the practical arrangements have been made (e.g.: is the room booked and confirmed?)

It is highly recommended that you not leave all of the above until the hour before your supervision! Competence includes effective time management skills and meeting deadlines. Field Work Supervisors want students to make effective use of supervision by taking a proactive approach to supervision.

SUMMARY

Supervision is an important component of field placement. There is differences between the supervision you will receive as a student versus as an employee in the field. It is important for you and your Field Work Supervisor to have an agreement around the expectation for your supervision. Effective preparation is a key element for making effective use of supervision.

OTHER FORMS OF SUPERVISION

20

The majority of students will experience one to one supervision with their Field Work Supervisor on placement. However, there are other forms of supervision which you may experience during your placement, this chapter will briefly explore group supervision and peer supervision.

Group Supervision

Group supervision is a common method of supervision used in the Field Integration Seminar. Most human service programs require that you attend a Field Integration Seminar while on field placement. The seminar typically consists of a group of 8 to 10 students and one Faculty Advisor for the duration of the field placement. Each student will have Field Work Supervisor and the students will all be in different placement sites. The students will meet together as a group with the Faculty Advisor for group supervision. The group sessions will generally cover learning issues while students will have individual supervision sessions covering work accountability with their Field Work Supervisors. Group supervision has a number of advantages – for example, students learn a great deal from each other about practice in different settings.

There are undoubtedly a number of benefits to group supervision, but to get the most out of the session, you need to play your part. Morrison, (2005) states that members of group supervision sessions need to:

- come on time and stay throughout
- come prepared
- specify the support they want from the group
- bring relevant material and experience
- promote positive group processes and support group members to focus on the task
- challenge processes that undermine the group process
- stay engaged, even if they are not talking, noticing their feelings and thoughts
- use the group appropriately – not for personal therapy
- support others in looking at their work
- participate in action techniques

- accept that their feelings, perceptions and values are true for them, but not necessarily for others
- listen to constructive feedback, and give constructive feedback to others
- abide by the rules of the group, especially on confidentiality
- maintain the group's norms and boundaries

Peer Supervision

A number of practicum sites have begun to recognize the value of peer group supervision and people learning from each other and have started to employ peer supervision as a method to supplement individual supervision. The difference between peer supervision and group supervision generally is that in peer supervision "all participants are of equal status, deciding on the roles and functions of group members and the way in which the group will be structured. Group supervision, by contrast, includes a supervisor who is at a more advanced level of expertise and who may have some form of hierarchical authority" (Akhurst, 2006).

Making Use of a Range of Supervision

If you are in a traditional field placement setting where all of your supervision is individual sessions with your Field Work Supervisor, you might want to think about how you could benefit from other forms of supervision. While some programs of study may not offer a Field Integration Seminar with structured group supervision, you could, for example, find out if there are other students on placement close to you and organize a couple of group peer supervision sessions between you. It doesn't matter if you are all on different placements or at different stages of your learning – in fact, it can enhance learning if there is diversity within the group. You could talk to your Field Work Supervisor about whether they have links with other Field Work Supervisor where some group supervision sessions could be organized.

SUMMARY

Most of the time, field placement supervision involves individual sessions with Field Work Supervisor. These sessions can be supplemented by other forms of supervision and you should consider how you can organize group or peer supervision if you feel these may be beneficial to your learning.

RECORDING SUPERVISION 21

It is important that supervision is accurately documented. It is common practice for Field Work Supervisors and students to take turns in recording sessions, while some Field Work Supervisors might expect you to record all of your sessions (possibly in order to provide you with evidence of your program learning outcomes). Less commonly, some Field Work Supervisors may want to do all of the recording themselves.

The method of documenting should also be considered. Some Field Work Supervisors may make brief notes and complete the full record following the session. Others type the notes straight onto the computer during the session. There are advantages and disadvantages to any method used. The method of documenting should be discussed between you and your Field Work Supervisor to ensure that you are both comfortable with it. Some people find a supervision session where the notes are recorded straight onto a computer de-personalizing and lacking in eye contact, while others prefer this, so negotiate clearly with your Field Work Supervisor.

Some programs provide a structured format for supervision notes and others offer guidance on how to document the supervision session. Always check with your Faculty Advisor and Field Work Supervisors. Some practicum sites provide their own format which you will need to use.

It is important that whatever format is used, the notes should be sufficiently comprehensive to provide a clear record of:

- your learning experiences in relation to the goals and objectives identified in the Learning Contract
- your progress towards meeting the program learning outcomes required for completion of your program of study
- any advice and guidance which your Field Work Supervisor gives you
- any disagreements, concerns, and complaints

The notes should also be comprehensible to third parties and many programs require supervision notes to be included in your professional development portfolio as a method of demonstrating that you have met program learning outcomes. This means that the notes will be read by others at various stages of the evaluation process.

Records of supervision should always be agreed by both you and your Field Work Supervisor and these notes should be signed by both of you to demonstrate that they have been shared. In the case of any disagreements about the recording, this should be recorded in the notes. Both of you can make a separate record of your different perspectives, again with both sets shared and signed to indicate that they have been shared.

Whether notes are handwritten or typed is generally open to negotiation, although some programs and agencies have expectations that notes are typed. The format of recording must be discussed and agreed together and if you have any specific needs, these must be addressed in the format of the recording.

Another aspect to consider in terms of recording is what is recorded about clients. Many agencies expect a record to be kept on a client's file about discussion in supervision. This is good practice, as it helps workers new to a case to familiarize themselves with what has been discussed. It also enables clients to see what role supervision has played if they access their records. However, if your supervision notes are to go into your portfolio, it is important to consider issues of confidentiality in terms of what is included about clients. In honouring the confidentiality of clients, the names of clients should not be on student supervision records. Instead, all clients are identified through the use of an alphabetical code, for instance, A, B, C, as so on. Separate and brief records are made in the client's file to meet agency requirements on accountability. Check your field placement's policy about how they expect you to manage this dilemma and discuss the issue with your Field Work Supervisor.

SUMMARY

Documentation of supervision notes need to be agreed upon between you and your Field Work Supervisor. Confidentiality issues also need careful consideration.

KEY LEARNING POINTS: SECTION E

- Supervision is key to facilitating your learning and assessing your skills and abilities

- Supervision has a number of functions. These should all be balanced to ensure good quality supervision and positive experiences

- Supervision can take a number of forms but all students need to receive formal supervision with their Field Work Supervisors

- Supervision records are very important in field placement

- The practicalities of supervision should be considered by your Field Work Supervisors and agreed with you

- Good practice in supervision is a joint responsibility

- You get out of your field placement what you put into it!

DEMONSTRATING COMPETENCE

F

Students are required to demonstrate that they have met the program outcomes for their program of study. The SSW, CYW, DSW and other related human service programs of study are built on students meeting program outcomes through the successful completion of courses and a field placement. Upon the completing your program of study, you will have completed the educational requirements for application to the Ontario College of Social Work and Social Service Work, the Ontario Association of Child and Youth Workers and the Developmental Services Special Interest Group. This section explores the process of evaluation, how you are likely to be evaluated and how you will be able to demonstrate that you have met the outcomes for your program of study.

"While on placement, you are continuously judged – and rightly so! You are judged as a team member, as a representative of the agency, by your placement provider (and potential employee), as a student representing your College and as a 'potential' child and youth worker. You are judged by clients, colleagues, managers, other professionals, your Field Work Supervisors and mentors, your College, your peers, never mind by society as a whole! There is no getting away from that fact. This, inevitably, takes its toll!

My advice is to allow yourself to accept that this is a learning experience – and do not lose sight of that. There may be times when you feel you 'should know' or 'should respond immediately' but remind yourself that the placement is there to provide that knowledge – you cannot have the answers all of the time and are not expected to.

I was able to use supervision to discuss my own, at times, unrealistic expectations that I placed on myself. One of my biggest 'fears' was being observed – I would spend many hours happily discussing issues in a professional manner with clients, or taking on the role of chair within a professional meeting, but the moment somebody mentions 'observation' and my belief in my own ability began to 'waiver.' I felt comfortable enough to discuss my anxieties about observations within supervision which helped alleviate some of the concerns. Again, communication cannot be underestimated – also, the more observations you have, the easier it gets! "

– Anonymous CYW Student

THE CONTINUING COMPETENCE PROGRAM FOR SOCIAL WORK AND SOCIAL SERVICE WORKER

Across all disciplines, competence refers to being able to demonstrate that the knowledge, values and skills learned can be integrated into practice (Carraccio et al., 2002). The Ontario College of Social Work and Social Service Workers (OCSWSSW) have introduced a Continuing Competence Program to ensure members are able to demonstrate competence and an ongoing commitment to professional development. The purpose of the Continuing Competence Program is to promote quality assurance with respect to the practice of social work and social service work. The Ontario Association for Child and Youth Counsellors and Developmental Services Special Interest Group are both in the process of determining their continuing competence requirements for their members.

In accordance with the Registration Regulation made under the Social Work and Social Service Act, all members must provide evidence of continuing competence to practice social work and social service work (OCSWSSW, 2009). The OCSWSSW expects that all members remain current with knowledge and practice relevant to their area of professional practice as set out in the Standards of Practice; members are required to demonstrate their commitment to ongoing professional develop through an annual process outlined in the Continuing Competence Program.

The Steps Involved in the Continuing Competence Program

Step 1: Become familiar with the Continuing Competence Program

Step 2: Review your practice

Step 3: Complete the self-assessment tool

Step 4: Complete summary sheets

Step 5: Review your progress

Step 6: Submit your declaration annually

Continuing Competence Program Self-Assessment Tool and Professional Development Plan Documents can be downloaded at http://www.ocswssw.org/en/about_ccp.htm

While the program learning outcomes are uniform across all colleges in Ontario, how these outcomes are evaluated may differ from college to college. However, all graduates applying for registration with the Ontario College of Social Workers and Social Service Workers will be required to maintain records of a Professional Development Plan as part of their annual registration process.

You should be aware of the Standards of Practice and your Field Work Supervisor should provide you with feedback on which areas of the standards they will be working on with you.

SUMMARY

The Continuing Competence Program is a requirement of all Social Service Workers in Ontario. These competencies are aligned to the program standards used for your program of study. You and your Field Work Supervisor must ensure that you are familiar with which parts of the standards are applicable to your field placement.

COLLECTING EVIDENCE

23

Your program of study requires that you demonstrate that you have met the program outcomes in order to graduate. The Continuing Competence Program for Social Service Worker in the field is yet another form of demonstrating that you have the required competencies to work in the field. Competence based assessments are a common way of ensuring that people have the skills and abilities to work as a regulated professional. Competence based assessments involve four distinct stages:

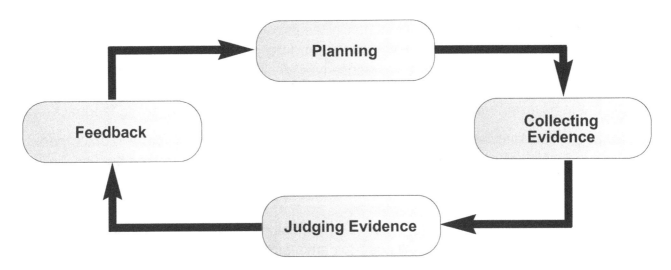

It is important to remember that these stages do not always occur in a neat sequence. It is quite common for Field Work Supervisors and students to be working on assessing several different program outcomes within all four stages of the process. Therefore, a number of the assessment cycles may be going on at the same time.

This cycle is summarized below. Additional details are explored in the following chapters, such as how you should go about collecting the necessary evidence.

√ *Planning*

It is vital that you and your Field Work Supervisor collaboratively work together to plan the assessment of your learning contract and that specific assessment activity (such as direct observations) are also well planned.

√ *Collecting Evidence*

It is your responsibility to identify the evidence you need to demonstrate that you have met the goals identified in your learning contract as well as the program outcomes for your program of study. You will need the support of your Field Work Supervisor. The evidence will be used to evaluate your performance when you are required to submit your professional development portfolio.

√ *Judging Evidence*

Your Field Work Supervisor and your Faculty Advisor assess tasks, assignments, projects, learning activities to ensure that you have evidence for your professional development portfolio.

√ *Feedback*

This is an essential aspect of the assessment cycle, which links the process of assessment to your learning. Your Field Work Supervisor will provide feedback to you on your performance in relation to your learning contract as well as through the mid-term and final evaluation. Your Faculty Advisor will provide feedback to you on the evidence collected throughout your field placement. This evidence typically is compiled into a final submission of your professional development portfolio. This will then lead on to planning the next stages of the assessment. Chapter 25 provides more information on receiving feedback.

Students may find matching their evidence of performance to program learning outcomes difficult, at least initially. You might know that you have done what is required but find providing evidence of this difficult (i.e., you know you have done something but can't *prove* that you have done it).

This chapter aims to give you a really clear way of thinking about how you should go about gathering the evidence which you will need to demonstrate your competence.

Sources of Evidence

The triangulation model below works well in terms of identifying the different sources of evidence.

Think about some of the work that you have done which relates to a particular outcome for your program of study, each corner of the triangle should be considered in terms of identifying relevant evidence of performance, for example:

*   *Observational Evidence of Practice* – can I arrange an observation of this work?
*   *Testimonial Evidence* – who has seen me do this and how can I get feedback from them?
*   *Product Evidence* – what record do I have of the work?

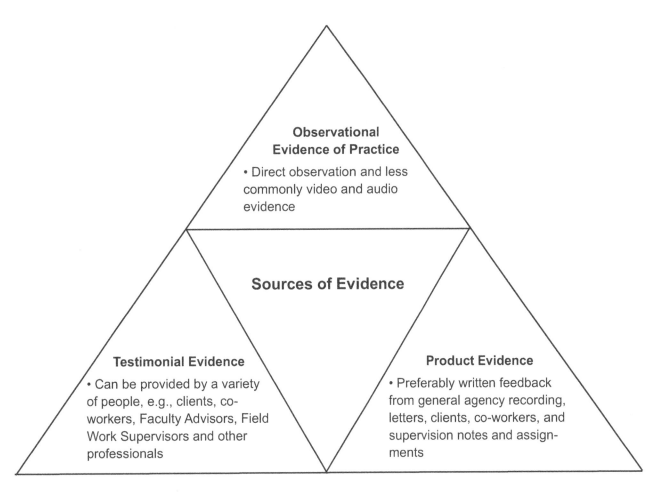

Observation is always the strongest source of evidence. However, it may not always be possible or appropriate for someone to observe certain areas of your practice. The two other corners of the triangle should then be considered.

Direct Observation

Direct observation always includes at least three parties: you, your Field Work Supervisor and the client or recipient of service whom you are working with. Each party has a different role to play in the observation. It is important to remember that where clients are involved, their needs take priority over yours or your Field Work Supervisors needs around your evaluation. It is important to remember that for you and your Field Work Supervisor this is a direct observation, for the client it is a meeting with a worker for an assessment or intervention to meet their needs.

The Potential of Direct Observation

Direct observation of practice has many benefits. It provides strong evidence for your Field Work Supervisor and Faculty Advisor around your competence. If they have witnessed you performing a specific task well, this can be reflected in your field placement evaluation with specific examples of what you did well and why. The following chart details the potential benefits and opportunities for you, the field work supervisor and the clients when a direct observation can be arranged during the field placement.

Benefits of Direct Observation		
Very Important	**Quite Important**	**Not Important**
• Allows you to reflect upon your skills and abilities • Allows for you to be able to document evidence of performance for your professional development portfolio • By having your Field Work Supervisor observe your work you can have him or her provide written feedback on your clinical skills • Allows for an opportunity to get immediate feedback on what your strengths and limitations may be • Allows for you to be proactive and to come up with a plan for developing skills and abilities	• Allows for a better understanding of what your current skills and abilities are and therefore can be useful in planning learning activities • It identifies areas for further work and an opportunity to provide relevant learning opportunities • Provides evidence of performance used for field placement evaluations	• Can act as a safeguard, through the scrutiny of your work by a more experienced practitioner (the Field Work Supervisor) • Could potentially improve the quality of service received as the client benefits from having two people provide service as opposed to only one • Empowers clients by providing them with an opportunity to evaluate the service received and give feedback to you

Practical Issues

Observations need to be carefully planned together with your Field Work Supervisor. Having a Field Work Supervisor witness your performance can cause you to feel anxious. In fact, everyone is anxious about their practice being observed. If you feel clear about what your Field Work Supervisor is looking for in an observation your anxiety is likely be reduced. This demonstrates the importance of thoughtful and effective assessment planning and more importantly allows for you to be transparent about the work you are doing with clients.

Remember that clients must always give permission for the observation. As a general rule you are responsible for getting permission from clients and explaining your Field Work Supervisor's role as an observer. Clients who have a good understanding of the observation process are less likely to be distracted or oppressed by the Field Work Supervisor's presence. It is important to remember that in any direct observation of practice, the presence of the observer (the Field Work Supervisor) is likely to have an impact on the situation. The more a client understands about the observer's role, the more effective the observation will go.

Top Tips for Direct Observations of Your Practice

- Make sure that the client has given consent and that they understand the observer's role
- Clarify the observation process with your Field Work Supervisor
- Share any concerns with your Field Work Supervisor
- Plan carefully
- Be clear about documentation requirements used at your practicum site for direct observations
- Be sure to plan a feedback session as soon as possible after the observation

A Collaborative Model of Direct Observation

A collaborative model of direct supervision would include a mutually agreed upon structure for feedback on the direct observation. Briefly, it involves careful planning before the observation when you and your Field Work Supervisor will each discuss the aims for the observation. For example, there may be some specific areas you would like your Field Work Supervisor to observe and he or she will discuss with you what they want to specifically observe.

Following the direct observation, the following questions may help guide a feedback discussion or debrief:

- Were the aims of the observation session achieved?
- What went well?
- What could have gone better?
- What would you do differently?
- What will you do in the future?

Both you and your Field Work Supervisor can share your thoughts using these broad areas. These simple headings provide a useful structure to guide debriefing and the direct observation experience. It can also help you to explore together whether there were any changes to the situation based on the presence of your Field Work Supervisor.

Putting structure to the direct observations is helpful for both students and Field Work Supervisors.

Video and Audio Evidence

Direct observation evidence can be supplemented by video or audio evidence of practice. Difficulties associated with video and audio evidence include:

- obtaining the necessary equipment
- ethical issues about videoing or audio taping clients and the associated confidentiality concerns
- many potential participants (clients and students) can find recordings uncomfortable

Since there are so many inherent difficulties it is recommend that video or audio evidence is used only in exceptional circumstances when discussed and agreed with the college, the agency, and all other parties involved.

Feedback from Others

Also referred to as third party feedback, testimonial evidence or witness testimony, this can be a strong source of evidence.

It is always important to negotiate the format of feedback with your Field Work Supervisor. On the whole, written feedback is preferable and some colleges provide forms for this.

Feedback can be obtained from a range of people:

Feedback from Clients

There can be obvious problems inherent in obtaining clients feedback for your evaluation. For example, the power dynamics of the client and student relationship can have a significant impact on the feedback which people feel able to give. Client feedback is a requirement of most programs of study, so you have to put some thought into the best way to obtain feedback. Obtaining client's feedback is important and should not be seen as purely something which has to be done to document your evidence of performance. Supervision that has been designed to gather client feedback may improve supervision, social worker performance and client outcomes (Alfred Kadushin & Harkness, 2002).

The format and methods for collecting client feedback may vary, so it is important to negotiate with your Field Work Supervisor as early as possible about how you will obtain client feedback. It may be appropriate for your Field Work Supervisor to seek feedback from clients following your direct observations, in which case you can discuss how this might best take place and what kinds of questions they might ask.

Some colleges provide specific guidance for obtaining client feedback and some even provide questionnaires to survey clients.

It can also be a useful learning experience to design your own form to give to clients to obtain feedback. This sounds like a fairly straightforward task, however, there is a great deal which you can learn from this task such as communication, client involvement and empowerment.

You need to think through the kinds of questions you want to ask on the form and how to word the questions. For example, would you use your name or "I" in the questions? The following question may be useful:

- Was the student reliable?
- Was the student respectful?
- Did the student keep you informed about their work with you?
- Did the student encourage you to make your own choices and decisions? How?
- What did you find useful about the way the student worked with you?
- How could the student have improved their work with you?

You could provide a few possible answers for the client to choose (i.e., a scale of satisfaction) for closed questions and invite comments for open questions. You might also want to make questions link specifically to a particular client's situation.

Of course, there may be situations where obtaining feedback from clients will be more difficult, for example, where clients do not communicate verbally. You could design a photographic or visual form which a client could complete with support. Those who know the client (e.g., an advocate, family members or friends) may be able to advise or provide feedback. Being creative is important in being able to obtain client feedback.

Feedback from Colleagues and other Professionals

Often, colleagues are in a better position to provide feedback on your practice. They may, for example, have worked alongside you on a specific piece of work related to outcomes in your program of study. Again, you might find it helpful to provide a questionnaire, or you could ask your colleagues to write some feedback about a specific aspect of your work they have witnessed. Other professionals who witness your performance can also be a good source of feedback.

General Guidance

Feedback is only helpful where it is clear and relevant to the criteria being assessed. It may be very pleasant for you to receive written feedback saying you are "a very good worker," but what exactly does that mean? Whoever seeks the feedback (usually you) needs to be very clear about what you are requesting, so that the evidence of performance relates directly to the criteria being evaluated.

Reflecting on Feedback

It is important that you look at feedback as a learning experience, not just an assessment method. This means you need to reflect on the feedback and draw some conclusions. This will be discussed more in the following chapter.

Product Evidence

Product evidence basically refers to anything that has been produced by you as part of your work.

You will routinely complete case notes, you may also write letters and reports. All of these can be strong sources of evidence. Your Field Work Supervisor should have routine access to agency documentation completed by you and this evidence should be discussed as part of the evaluation process.

Documentation produced specifically as part of the field placement experience, the integrative seminar or from your program of study, generally could also be used as product evidence, for example, reflective journals, assignments and supervision notes.

Using the Full Range of Available Evidence

As you progress through your placement, a whole range of evidence from the different sources discussed in this chapter will be available. Remember also that supervision discussion will provide evidence of your performance, so supervision notes provide a good source of product evidence.

It is important that you provide a wide range of evidence for your evaluation. This ensures that your evaluation is fair and that the opportunities for you to demonstrate your performance are maximized.

SUMMARY

A range of assessment methods and evidence sources can be used to help your Field Work Supervisor and Faculty Advisor in assessing your performance. The triangulation model can be useful as it shows you why different sources of evidence are important. Fair and reliable evaluations will involve the use of a wide range of assessment methods. You must feel confident about providing evidence – finding the evidence is not your Field Work Supervisor's role – it's yours.

THE IMPORTANCE OF FEEDBACK

24

Feedback is intrinsically linked to your evaluation in two main ways:

1. You should seek feedback from a variety of sources as part of being able to demonstrate that you have met the outcomes for your program of study

2. Your Field Work Supervisor and Faculty Advisor will provide you with feedback on the evidence you have presented

Feedback can be either positive (that is, re-enforcing good practice) or negative (that is, feedback on poor performance). Both positive and negative feedback can be constructive. Where feedback is constructive it will enable you to develop your skills and abilities. Where feedback is missing or destructive you will not be able to develop effectively.

Feedback is a vital part of the assessment cycle in that if your Field Work Supervisor assesses that you are "not yet competent," then feedback will enable you and your Field Work Supervisor to review and adapt your evaluation plan. Even when you are judged to be competent, feedback is still a vital part of the process as this will enable you to plan for your future development beyond the end of the field placement. It is important that you never feel that once you have graduated, you have no more to do. The achievement of any qualification is always part of a continuum of professional development.

Constructive Feedback

Constructive feedback provides information about your performance against the outcomes for your program of study so that you can maintain a positive attitude towards yourself, your placement, and the qualification you are attempting to achieve. Constructive feedback should be:

- *Positive*

Good quality feedback should always begin and end with a positive comment. This is often referred to as the positive sandwich. The content of the sandwich gives the receiver of the feedback something to work on, while the slices of bread are the positive aspects. In this way, your self-esteem and motivation are likely to be strengthened.

- *Specific*

Feedback should be specific and deal with specific instances related to performance. Making generalizations or sweeping statements is not helpful to making improvements with performance. For example, *"when asking about mobility, you moved too quickly through the questions rather than allowing the person to fully answer,"* rather than *"your listening skills were poor."*

- ### *Objective*

Feedback should use objective rather than subjective terms. For example, *"my perception was that when you repeated the same question several times the person became confused,"* rather than *"your questioning technique was confusing."*

- ### *Actionable*

Feedback should be directed towards performance that you can do something about. For example, *"if you slowed down your delivery, it would probably be easier for the person to follow what you were saying,"* rather than *"your accent is hard to understand."*

- ### *Prioritized*

Feedback should concentrate on the two or three key areas for improvement, preferably including those where you can manage making changes in a timely manner. Issues should be broken down into smaller, step-by-step goals.

- ### *Offer alternatives*

Feedback should offer you suggestions to what could have been done differently and turn negatives into positives. For example, *"when you remained seated at the start it seemed unwelcoming. Shaking her hand and smiling would have helped set up a better rapport."*

- ### *Well-timed*

The most useful feedback is given when you are receptive to it and it is sufficiently close to the event when it occurred.

- ### *Facilitative*

Rather than prescribing performance, feedback should help you to question your performance and encourage you to develop reflective practice. For example, *"How might that have been interpreted by the client?"*

- ### *Clear and Concise*

Feedback should avoid jargon wherever possible and the communication should be clear. Your Field Work Supervisor should check that you understand the feedback which they have shared.

You have a right to receive constructive feedback from your Field Work Supervisor during your placement. However, as you know, rights are always balanced with responsibilities and in this context your responsibility is to receive and decide how to use it.

Receiving Feedback

Accepting and receiving feedback is a vital skill which you will be expected to have from the beginning of your field placement. It is widely accepted that being able to "receive feedback gracefully is a career enhancing skill which is greatly valued by employers" (King, 2007).

Receiving feedback is an excellent learning opportunity. This learning is maximized when the feedback is constructive. The feedback process will only be constructive if the person receiving the feedback has developed the necessary skills in receiving feedback. When receiving feedback at any stage in your placement, work towards the following:

> **Top Tips for Receiving Feedback**
> - Be open and positive
> - Listen actively
> - Focus on your reactions
> - Make sure you understand the feedback
> - Make notes
> - Don't take criticism personally
> - Reflect on your learning
> - Use the feedback to enhance your practice

- *Maintain an open attitude*

Don't be defensive or defend yourself. This may sound easy, but it can be difficult to do. If you find yourself feeling defensive about a piece of feedback, you need to remind yourself that the reality is that a defensive reaction to feedback generally results from it being accurate!

- *Employ your active listening skills*

Listen actively, look at the person providing feedback and maintain an open body language.

- *Clarify the feedback*

Ask any questions you need to in order to make sure you understand the feedback.

- *Recognize the giver of the feedback*

Providing feedback is not an easy task. Your Field Work Supervisor is likely to have put a great deal of thought into the feedback. It takes a great deal of time and effort to provide thoughtful feedback. It is advisable to thank the person giving you feedback, for example, "you've really given me something to think about, thanks!" This will demonstrate your commitment to learning and it will help you to maintain a positive and open attitude.

- *Write down the feedback*

Try to write down what was said as soon as possible. You will find this assists with your reflection later.

- ### *Don't take criticism personally*

Feedback is a professional process. Recognize that part of being a professional is learning from how others perceive you.

- ### *Recognize learning*

Remember that simply because someone has picked up on an area of your practice which can be improved, this does not mean you will fail your placement or that you won't do well in the field. Even the very best worker can improve on some aspect of their practice.

- ### *Reflect*

If some aspect of the feedback puzzles you, take some time to reflect. How might the person's perception have been formed?

- ### *Focus*

Make sure that you are not distracted so that you can focus fully on the feedback. Stay present and try to truly understand the meaning behind the feedback. Try to avoid framing a response in your mind until you have heard all of the feedback.

- ### *Recognize your reactions*

Notice your own reactions and how the feedback makes you feel. Sometimes it helps to partially disassociate yourself and imagine you are a "fly on the wall" witnessing feedback being given to someone else. This can help you to think the feedback through objectively, rather than emotionally.

Rich (2009) suggests that in receiving feedback, people take either a negative (closed) style or a positive (open) style. The table of the following page summarizes the negative and positive style.

As a SSW, CYW or DSW you will no doubt need to give feedback to clients at some point in your career. The more well developed your skills in receiving feedback, the better positioned you will be to give feedback. You should not underestimate the importance of developing your skills in this area.

To illustrate the importance of you developing and demonstrating skills in this area, it might be worth pointing out that it is not uncommon for students on field placement to rationalize or become defensive when receiving feedback despite the feedback being balanced with strengths and areas for improvement. So while these students may be progressing well in their field placement, the defensive style may undermine the supervision process and one's ability to provide evidence of performance. Ultimately, a defensive response to feedback could result in failing a field placement as students need to be able to able to receive feedback on their performance in the field placement as well as throughout their career.

Negative / Closed	Positive / Open
Defensive: defends actions, objects to feedback	Open: listens without frequent interruption or objection
Attacking: turns the table on the person providing feedback	Responsive: willing to truly "hear" what is being said
Denies: refutes the accuracy or fairness of the feedback	Accepting: accepts the feedback without denial
Disrespectful: devalues the person giving the feedback	Respectful: recognizes the value of the feedback
Closed: ignores the feedback	Engaged: interacts appropriately seeking clarification where needed
Inactive listening: makes no attempt to understand the meaning of the feedback	Active listening: listens attentively and tries to understand the meaning of the feedback
Rationalizing: finds explanations for the feedback that dissolve personal responsibility	Thoughtful: tries to understand the personal behaviour that has led to the feedback
Superficial: listens and agrees but does not act on the feedback	Sincere: genuinely wants to make changes and learn

When Feedback is Difficult

Feedback on performance can be difficult for a range of reasons. However, it is vital that you receive honest feedback throughout your field placement learning opportunity.

What do I do if I disagree with the feedback from my Field Work Supervisor or Faculty Advisor?

This can be problematic as you won't be able to move on through the process of evaluation until there is some level of agreement.

If you disagree with the feedback, then:

- ask for specific detailed examples
- clarify each other's version of events and have an open mind
- you should discuss together as to what action will be taken in order to explore this further or how agreement can be reached

- clarify exactly what you need to do about the feedback – do you need to provide more evidence of performance and what is expected of you in terms of action?

What do I do if I feel upset by the feedback?

Receiving negative feedback can be really hard, so if you feel upset:

- try not to get angry as this will not help your Field Work Supervisor, Faculty Advisor or you. Take a break and don't worry about crying as it can relieve stress
- talk about why you find the feedback upsetting
- try not to put off the session. Try to move on instead to finding solutions together which will end the session on a positive note.

SUMMARY

Providing good quality constructive feedback is a skill (which Field Work Supervisors and Faculty Advisors need to work hard to develop and keep under review). Being able to accept and reflect on feedback is an equally important skill (which you might need to develop). Some people do not like hearing positive feedback, and most people can struggle with negative feedback. If you are complimented, accept it! If the feedback is negative, it is important that you clarify what you are expected to do and then decide how to integrate this feedback into your practice.

COMPLETING THE FINAL EVALUATION

25

So far this section has considered how to go about identifying appropriate evidence of your performance. What has not been considered so far is how this final evaluation is recorded and completed.

Every college will have their own system of documentation, although most colleges have:

- a format for recording the observations of your practice
- a format or final evaluation for your final report (and if applicable, a mid-placement report)

It is important that you use the documentation provided by your college and that you follow whatever requirements your program of study has identified. Programs vary in their requirements about:

- which aspects of the program outcomes you will need to demonstrate in the field placement and which outcomes will be demonstrated through course work.
- what academic work (e.g., assignments and analysis of practice) you will need to complete as part of the field placement process
- how observations of your practice will be carried out and how these will be evaluated.
- what documentation needs to be completed as part of the evaluation (e.g., mid-placement report, final report, and professional development portfolio) and the extent to which you are expected to contribute
- what has to be provided at the end of a placement (e.g., Is a portfolio required? What should the portfolio contain? Do you have academic work such as an analysis of your practice to complete? What is the deadline for this work? Who marks this – your Faculty Advisor, Field Work Supervisor or both?)
- Other assessment requirements (e.g., some programs require client feedback to be specifically recorded).

You must ensure that you follow all of your program's requirements. It will be clear by now that a range of documentation is produced during the field placement.

All of the documentation generated during a placement will be useful in completing your evaluation and ensuring that students provide clear evidence of performance in relation to the outcomes for their program of study.

Professional Development Portfolios

Many programs of study have moved to using a professional development portfolio to document student performance and competence in meeting program outcomes. Typically this is done in conjunction with a final evaluation report. Professional development portfolios identify how the student is able to integrate theory, action, self-reflection, group learning, and assessment – the essential elements of a professional education for students entering the human service field. Emerging research in social work education suggests that portfolios can help students learn how to learn and to develop their identities as maturing professionals (Alvarex & Moxley, 2004; Schatz, 2004; Schatz & Simon, 1999).

Portfolios are traditionally viewed as a personal collection of information and artifacts that describe and document a person's achievements, evidence of performance and learning. The most common use of a portfolio is to compile and demonstrate a person's work as part of an application process for employment. Increasingly, however, portfolios are now being used as a final measure of evaluation for the completion of an education program.

Keeping track of your performance is useful for a number of reasons:

- It allows you to link what you have learned in the classroom with your practical experience on field placement

- It can address any anxieties you have about gathering evidence of your performance

- Your ownership of the assessment process is enhanced and self-evaluation and reflection are encouraged

- It encourages ongoing discussion of your performance which can help you to identify further sources of evidence

- As evidence of performance is recorded on an ongoing basis during the placement, this will save time for you and your Field Work Supervisor when the final report evaluation needs to be produced.

- Ongoing completion can help to identify where the gaps in learning goals and objectives may be early on so that you may be proactive in ensuring that these needs can be addressed early on in the placement.

For programs of study that do not require a final submission of a professional development portfolio, it is strongly recommended that you use some way of tracking your performance in relation to the outcomes of your program. It can be as simple as the following table.

You can then complete this as the placement progresses and it can be used to form the basis of discussion about assessment in supervision. The completed record will also be helpful to the Field Work Supervisor in completing the final report as it aligns with evidence based outcomes.

Program Outcome	Assessment Plan	Evidence of Performance	Evaluation Decision	Further Evidence Required

The Final Evaluation

Your Field Work Supervisor will need to complete a final evaluation at the end of your placement. This final evaluation can then provide you with an effective tool for identifying your future learning needs and for providing you with examples of successful practice for use in future placements, job applications and interviews (see section H for more detail).

Final evaluations will always conclude with the Field Work Supervisor's recommendation on whether you have passed or failed the placement. This is clearly the aspect of practice learning which creates the most anxiety for students. It is vital that nothing in the final evaluation comes as a surprise to you. You should be kept aware of the progress of the assessment, your Field Work Supervisor's judgments and how these will inform the final recommendation at all stages of the placement. You should be involved in the completion of the final evaluation and it is usual that this is an agenda item in supervision for the final few weeks of the placement. You must also read the evaluation prior to its submission and you should sign it to show that the report has been shared with you.

Students are typically required to complete a self-evaluation as well. It is not uncommon for students to self evaluate the goals and objective in their learning contract and also complete a self evaluation of their performance in relation to the outcomes for their program of study. You and your Field Work Supervisor would then meet to compare and review the Field Work Supervisors final evaluation and your self evaluation.

Many programs require a mid-placement evaluation to be provided for a meeting mid-way through the placement (usually attended by you, your Faculty Advisor, your Field Work Supervisor and where applicable, your supervisor). The mid-term field placement evaluation will give an indication of your progress to date and issues to be addressed in the second half of the placement. It should also indicate whether you are on track to pass the placement. Again, it may be required for you to self evaluate at this time and compare this with your Field Work Supervisors evaluation.

Contents of the Professional Development Portfolios

Most programs require you to submit some kind of portfolio at the completion of the field placement. Portfolios vary significantly, although they generally bring together evidence of performance, sometimes supported by actual exhibits. They often contain reflection and documents generated across the field placement. Typical contents include:

- Learning Contract
- Mid-term Field Placement Evaluation
- Final Field Placement Evaluation
- Supervision notes
- Student reflections
- Academic work completed during the placement and throughout the entire program of study
- Examples of practice - such as letters (see confidentiality below)
- Reflections and assignment completed through the Field Integration Seminar
- Feedback from others
- Reports on direct observations of practice

It is important that you, your Field Work Supervisor, and your Faculty Advisor and are all clear from the beginning of the placement about portfolio requirements. Students can often become very anxious about the production of a portfolio unless they are clear about both the content and structure. Your Field Work Supervisor will need to familiarize themselves with portfolio requirements so that they are clear on their responsibilities and what they need to produce.

Confidentiality

There are a range of confidentiality issues in relation to the evaluation of your performance. It is obviously vital that the names and other identifying features of clients and families do not appear in any documentation or in your professional development portfolio. Programs should provide guidance on how they expect confidentiality to be maintained, but the most straightforward method is to use an alphabetical code.

Where portfolios require actual evidence of practice to be included (e.g., completed agency documentation and letters written by you), it is vitally important to ensure that the evidence is fully and appropriately completed honouring anonymity of clients. Agency requirements on confidentiality and data protection must be considered. If you fail to address issues of confidentiality you are directly contravening the required outcomes of your program of study.

Evaluation Process Following Field Placement

Many people feel that when the final field placement evaluation is completed and submitted along with any other required documentation (e.g., portfolio), the evaluation process is complete. However, at this stage the Field Work Supervisors recommendation is still just that – a recommendation. The final evaluation process within the college needs to be completed. The general framework is as follows:

1. Final evaluation by Field Work Supervisor. Recommendations of pass or fail of the field placement.

2. Final evaluation by student (student self-evaluates performance of the field placement)

3. Completion of all field integration assignments. Recommendations of pass or fail of the field placement.

4. Submission of professional development portfolio to facualty advisor.

5. Faculty Advisor submits the final decision of a pass or fail of the field placement.

6. Similarly, completion of the CYW and DSW program and application to register with the respective regulatory body.

SUMMARY

All Colleges will have their own specific requirements for the completion of the evaluation of the Field Placement. It is important that you are familiar with this and feel confident about what will happen and when.

MANAGING ENDINGS

26

Significant time and energy is put into placement preparation and establishing you in a successful placement. It is also important to devote some time to planning an effective ending. It can be helpful for you to give some thought as to how you want to end your time with the clients and staff that you have worked with. This can be important as it can also affect whether the practicum site will offer placements to other students in the future.

Learning to manage endings can also be an important skill for graduates who wish to pursue work in short-term service settings, such as initial assessment teams, homeless shelters or child protection work, where fast paced contract work can mean your involvement with clients can be relatively brief.

A final placement meeting generally takes place between you, your Faculty Advisor, your Field Work Supervisor and on-site supervisor (where applicable). This facilitate an effective ending for you. This meeting will cover your final evaluation, your professional development portfolio, and your future learning needs.

Evaluating the Practicum Site

It is important that every placement is fully evaluated. Many programs provide specific field placement evaluation tools, which may be discussed at this meeting or you may be asked to complete a feedback questionnaire following the end of the placement. Students, Faculty Advisors, Field Work Supervisor and Supervisors should all be involved in evaluating the placement. This is not about evaluating or assessing you, but is about evaluating the quality of the placement, the opportunities provided, the learning opportunities, and supervision.

Field Work Supervisors and Supervisors should use this opportunity to receive feedback on the field placement learning environment and on their skills. Learning from the evaluation should help your Field Work Supervisor and Supervisor (where relevant) to improve the placement and their own skills for the future. It may be helpful for you to think about the following areas before your final meeting:

- The range of learning opportunities you have been offered
- The extent to which these learning opportunities met your learning goals and objectives
- The job shadowing opportunities provided by staff

- Any issues in meeting the program learning outcomes and how you have addressed these issues
- The support and learning opportunities you have been offered through supervision
- Any issues around health and safety
- Any ideas for the field placement setting in working with students in the future

It is important to consider ideas which you might want to discuss at this meeting, so that any issues you have faced can be shared constructively in order to improve the field placement learning opportunity for future students.

Managing Endings with Clients

During a longer placement, you are likely to have built up effective working relationships with clients. Managing how you will say goodbye and move on positively is as important as all of the engagement skills in first meeting with somebody and contracting how your working relationship should operate. Many clients need to be clear as to why you are moving on, and clarifying these timeframes clearly from the start is important in any student placement.

Most employers and placement settings will have policies on giving and receiving gifts, and it is really important that you consider these and issues outlined by your professional regulatory body around professional practice. Moving on in a professional capacity is usually about supporting the client to review and own the progress they have made from the time they first requested or were referred to services, and not about you and the work you have done. Think about how you plan to empower the clients, families or groups that you may have worked with throughout your field placement. Setting aside time to allow clients to have ownership of their own progression or "distance travelled" is an important step in termination.

For some people, a pictorial representation or use of another tool such as a "change chart" can be helpful as a document which they can keep and reflect on. For others, reviewing an initial assessment or service plan, possibly via a multiagency progress review, can be effective in ensuring that all of the professionals involved share an agreement over the progress that has been made. Other clients may need to have their case transferred to another worker in the agency, and lots of students will spend time in supervision and discussion with Field Work Supervisors, Supervisors and colleagues as the end of the placement approaches considering ways in which this transfer can be achieved positively.

Other Endings

Hopefully, your relationships with the staff and with your Field Work Supervisor will have also been positive, so it is worth considering how you want to say goodbye to these key people. Some people have strong feelings about avoiding long protracted goodbyes, staying in touch, goodbye celebrations, collections for presents and other key issues in colleague relationships. Many of these factors are influenced by the impact of the culture within the agency you have been placed with. It is really worthwhile to check out how people work before making assumptions or decisions about how endings should work for you.

SUMMARY

A great deal of work goes into preparing for a placement. It is important to recognize, however, that placement endings are also important. You will need to put thought into ending your placement positively. Managing endings is an important aspect of your learning.

ADDRESSING DIFFICULTIES IN FIELD PLACEMENT

G

Field placement is generally a positive experience for all involved. However, occasionally problems of various kinds do occur. This section considers how difficulties can be explored and addressed, and offers guidance on what to do if you find yourself facing problems in your placement.

ADDRESSING PROBLEMS IN FIELD PLACEMENT

27

Field placement is generally a very positive experience for everyone involved, however, at times problems or difficult issues can occur. It is easy to see the potential for conflict or other difficulties if you consider the number of people potentially involved in a field placement.

While it is not possible to consider all of the potential problems that can occur in field placement, consideration will be given to situations which could be thought of as "problematic."

The following questions are designed to help you consider strategies to deal with a variety of situations where things could go wrong during your placement. Perhaps you might need to talk to your Field Work Supervisor about working together to design a new, more effective way of managing your field placement or working with you. Whatever difficulty you might be experiencing, it is worth reflecting on these questions as a starting point.

√ *Power and Powerlessness*

Have you discussed some of the issues and feelings you might be experiencing around power imbalances openly with your Field Work Supervisor?
See Chapter 5.

√ *Roles and Responsibilities*

Is everyone's role and responsibility clear? With off-site supervision arrangements, are the arrangements in place and working in terms of the three way relationship (between you, your Field Work Supervisor and On-site Supervisor)?
See Chapter 3.

√ *Placement Preparation*

Did you prepare effectively for the placement? Has everyone been prepared fully for the field placement process? Do the people in your agency, organization or institution all understand your role and what is expected of you as a student?
See Section C.

√ *Learning Contract and Program Requirements*

Is the learning contract clear about what is expected of you? Was this negotiated clearly with your Field Work Supervisor and Faculty Advisor? Do you have a clear set of ground rules? Is there a clear evaluation plan? Is there a comprehensive plan for your learning? Have all of these been kept under review and updated as necessary? Have you kept your

side of the learning contract?
See Chapter 2.

√ *Specific Needs*

Have you identified any specific needs which you have? Have you discussed and shared these openly with your Field Work Supervisor?
See Chapter 11.

√ *Taking Responsibility*

Are you taking an active approach to your placement? Are you taking responsibility for your own learning? Or are you taking the role of passive recipient?
See Section D.

√ *Program Requirements*

Do you fully understand how your performance will be evaluated? Have you sought advice and support from relevant people?
See Chapter 22.

√ *The Evaluation Process*

Have you worked through the evaluation process in a systematic way and come to an agreement with your Field Work Supervisor about how you will gather evidence of your performance, how this will be assessed, and how you would like to receive feedback?
See Chapter 23.

√ *Evaluation Methods*

Have you gathered sufficient evidence to demonstrate that you have met the outcomes for your program of study? Does the evidence show your skills and abilities against the elements of performance required for your program of study?
See Chapter 24.

√ *Opportunities*

Have you benefited from sufficient learning opportunities to demonstrate competence? What can you do to raise the need for a greater range of opportunities to be provided if you are concerned?
See Chapter 17.

√ *Feedback*

Have you been given clear, constructive feedback and reflected on the feedback?
See Chapter 25.

SUMMARY

Reflecting on your practice in situations where things are "going wrong" in field placement can help to identify a solution and an action plan for getting back on track.

WHAT TO DO IF YOU ARE FAILING A PLACEMENT

28

Field Work Supervisors want students to have positive field placement learning experiences and pass their placements. However, ultimately your Field Work Supervisor and Faculty Advisor's responsibility is to safeguard the long term future of the social work and social service work profession:

> Practice teachers have an individual and collective responsibility to ensure that qualifying social workers are competent to practice. This requires a vigorous assessment of competence and a willingness to contribute to the ongoing development of social work education at a local and national level (NOPT, 2004).

Unfortunately, on some occasions students do fail to provide evidence that they have met the outcomes for their program of study. Consequently, if you fail to meet the outcomes of your program, you will not qualify for registration with your professional regulatory body. In such situations, generally students fall into one of two categories:

- Marginal – essentially a marginal student is one who may be referred to as "borderline." If by the mid-point of the placement your Field Work Supervisor isn't able to answer the question "is this student on target to pass the placement?" with some confidence, then you could be considered marginal.

- Failing – where students are failing, it should be clearer to identify than when a student is marginal. It may be clear that you are not demonstrating competence if you are practicing in a way which directly contravenes the required outcomes of your program of study.

Marsh et al. (2005) state that concerns about failing students generally relate to:

- poor communication and interpersonal skills
- lack of interest and failure to participate in field placement
- persistent lateness
- lack of personal insight
- lack of insight into professional boundaries

Failing students usually exhibit a combination of these characteristics. In addition, there are other obvious areas where students fail, such as disrespectful, oppressive or dangerous practice.

Other examples include:

- lack of reflection or not demonstrating reflective practice (e.g., not competing a reflective journal or not reflecting and acting on feedback)
- poor professional boundaries with clients. An example of this might be student socializing with a client outside of field placement
- not making effective use of supervision (e.g., being late, not preparing sufficiently or not completing actions which you have agreed to)
- allowing personal issues to get in the way of your work on placement
- not challenging unethical practice in others – it is an expectation that you would go directly to your Field Work Supervisor and Faculty Advisor if you witnessed staff or co-workers acting unethical or immoral.

If any concerns are raised with you, it is your responsibility to seek clarification if you do not understand or agree with the concerns. Some of the above items are quite subjective and different people will have different ideas on what positive use of supervision constitutes, so you need to be absolutely clear on:

- what evidence your Field Work Supervisor may be using to evaluate your ability to make effective use of supervision
- how you need to address this concern
- what is expected and by when
- what will happen next
- what will happen if you do not provide the necessary evidence

When concerns are raised, it is important that an action plan is created together with your Field Work Supervisor. Your Faculty Advisor may also need to be involved when there is disagreement over any concerns. A sample action plan is provided on the next page.

What are the concerns and what is expected?	What does the student need to do to address concerns?	What support is available for the student?	Timeframes: when should this change be achieved by?
• Assessments not completed on time. Client needs to be assessed within 7 days of allocation.	• Complete assessments for clients C, D and E.	• Take one case off the workload. • Assessments to be checked by the team manager and Field Work Supervisor and specific detailed feedback to be provided. • Informal support is available from the Field Work Supervisor between supervision sessions.	• These 3 assessments to be completed satisfactorily by next Friday. • Next assessment to be completed within 7 days of allocation.
• Student has been late for supervision and has not prepared tasks which have been agreed.	• Student needs to be on time for each session. • Student and Field Work Supervisor will review all actions set at the end of each session. • Student needs to complete each action which is agreed and notify the Field Work Supervisor the day before supervision if emergencies arise. • Evidence of specific outcomes is needed by next supervision.	• Workload relief as above. • Additional support from Field Work Supervisor is available between sessions. • Student can contact college for additional support.	• Change is expected by the next supervision and should be maintained for each subsequent supervision session.

Support can come from a range of sources, but we would suggest that many students find that the most valuable support might come from peers or from within their Field Integration Seminar group. As discussed in Section A, colleagues and others who are involved in your placement are also involved in your evaluation, so it is important that you do not impede this further by drawing staff into your difficulties. This is likely to frustrate the team manager, especially if they are not your Field Work Supervisor and they do not have regular contact with you. You do not want to have feedback given to your Field Work Supervisor that you are impacting staff morale negatively.

As discussed in Chapter 25, it is important that you consider the importance of responding to concerns quickly and effectively and that you do not respond aggressively or defensively if concerns are raised. However, it is fine to clarify and discuss the issues openly, and it is right that you should seek a full understanding about the nature of any concerns.

Remember that early in the placement the expectation may be different then what would be expected of you later in the placement. This means that what is expected of you in terms of your performance and competence is rightly expected to increase as you progress through your program of study.

Procedures

Colleges will all have clear guidelines when a student is identified as failing or marginal. Each program will differ, but as a general requirement where there are concerns, these procedures should be invoked as soon as possible. Most procedures are identified in your Field Placement Manual. Typically, the student or Field Supervisor will be in contact with the Faculty Advisor to identify the concerns.

A meeting will be held involving you, your Faculty Advisor, your Field Work Supervisor and possibly the Supervisor (where relevant). The concerns and each person's perspective on these procedures will be discussed in detail. All forms of documentation will be taken into account. The outcome of the meeting typically involves an action plan outlining how the concerns will be addressed specifically. Many colleges require that the student sign a behavioral contract detailing what will be done, by whom and when. A follow-up meeting or conference call will typically follow to ensure that corrective action has taken place. The college may have a format for an action plan, or you may use something similar to the example on the previous page.

You must ensure that you are familiar with the procedures in place for your program of study. These will be discussed and agreed in your pre-placement meeting and everyone, including you, should be confident about the procedures and in what circumstances they might be instigated.

The Benefit of the Doubt?

Beginning concerns procedures can evoke many difficult emotions for all parties involved. Most people would agree that if you are not able to demonstrate that you have met the outcomes for your program of study, you should not pass the placement. Failing a field placement would prevent you from graduating which consequently prevents you from meeting the registration requirements for your professional regulating body.

The other issue for you if you end up in this situation is that although having concerns raised in this way is upsetting and stressful, it is better that you have the chance to work on them now. The alternative is that you do not change certain practices and consequently this would continue in future placements and in your job.

> **Top Tips if You are Struggling on Placement**
> - Keep Calm
> - Clarify concerns
> - Work in partnership to create an action plan
> - Locate and use appropriate support
> - Make sure you understand relevant procedures
> - Clarify the potential outcomes
> - Don't see it as the end of the world! Use the process to enhance your learning

The problem with giving you the benefit of the doubt might be that this potentially sets you up to fail when you might be able to develop considerably with appropriate action planning. Remember, nobody wants you to fail, but it is up to you to do the work which you need to achieve in order to pass the field placement. Concerns procedures should be viewed positively and action planning processes can really support you to develop your practice. In many cases where concerns procedures are instigated, students go on to successfully pass their field placement.

Recognizing and Addressing Emotional Issues

Stress can have an impact on both you and your Field Work Supervisor, and if concerns are raised, then this is likely to affect the relationship between you.

This illustrates why it is important for you to receive additional support when concerns are being addressed. The college should be able to advise students on where you can obtain support from. The agency, organization or institution which employs the Field Work Supervisor should be able to offer support to them.

Possible Outcomes

As stated, one of the outcomes that can result from following concerns procedures is that you may develop considerably and go on to the pass the placement. However, in some circumstances, students may fail to meet the outcomes of their program of study by the end of the placement. Various options are then possible:

- You may be asked to repeat a placement in a new field placement environment. This may give you the opportunity to develop further and to ultimately pass the program of study

- Sometimes, you may be given the opportunity to transfer into another related academic program that does not involve a field placement, such as a diploma in one of the general arts and sciences programs

- Sometimes students defer a year, obtain additional experience and repeat the failed placement

Failing a placement should not be considered as a "disaster" for your future. Indeed, if you passed and you were really not ready to enter the field, you might be "set up to be fired" in your future career. There are potentially a number of positive outcomes for you in this situation.

Some students who have failed their field placement and have stepped out of their program of study for a year have returned to the program and have been successful in future field placements. These students have worked hard to ensure that their personal life has become more manageable and consequently become successful in their subsequent field placement, therefore, allowing them to graduate and qualify for registration with their regulating body.

SUMMARY

Most students progress well in field placement environments and pass the placement. However, sometimes difficulties will occur. If this happens to you, it is important that you discuss concerns openly and take appropriate action to address the concerns which have been raised.

KEY LEARNING POINTS: SECTION G

- Problems should not occur if roles and responsibilities have been clarified at the start of your placement and you are clear on what is expected of you.

- Where problems do occur, you should make sure you are clear about what you need to do in order to resolve the situation.

- Open discussion is vital to make sure problems are dealt with as early in the placement as possible.

- It is your responsibility to make the most of whatever placement you are offered.

- You get out of practice learning what you put into it!

BEYOND FIELD PLACEMENT

This section considers what happens after you complete your final placement. Learning should be something that is life-long for all of us. The section also considers applying for jobs, and the post qualifying framework used in Ontario for SSWs, CYWs, DSWs, and other related human service workers.

IDENTIFYING YOUR FUTURE LEARNING NEEDS

29

At the end of your final placement, you may have a mixture of feelings. Some of these feelings may be relief at having the placement finished and your final evaluation completed. You may be experiencing a combination of emotions, feeling excited and apprehensive about entering the field.

When you are considering what your individual learning needs are for going into employment, it is helpful to consider the following points.

Revisiting the Bring-and-Buy Exercise and the Confidence Checklist

This might be an enjoyable exercise as well as one which is useful for you in identifying what your current learning needs are following the completion of your field placement. These two exercises may provide you with an opportunity to reflect back on your growth and development throughout your placement. Looking at the ideas you generated at the start of a placement should show you the areas where you feel you have changed and identify how you have learned from the experiences, as well as give you ideas for what you want to "buy" from your first position in the field or your next field placement. The confidence checklist can show you the progress you have made, and your Field Work Supervisor should be able to consider with you the areas where you may still feel you need to continue in developing confidence.

Using the Final Report

Your Field Work Supervisor will be responsible for making recommendations about your future learning needs in the final report. However, it is not just their responsibility, it is also your responsibility to identify and discuss your learning needs for the future; this should be shared with your Field Work Supervisor during your final supervision sessions.

Be Specific!

As discussed in Chapter 11, your learning goals and objectives should be specific in order for them to be actionable. When you create a professional development portfolio, this portfolio will help you prepare for employment interviews, it will help you as part of the probationary requirements that many employers have with new employees as well as help you in maintaining your registration with your regulating body.

SUMMARY

At the end of your final placement, you should be able to identify what professional development would be beneficial for you moving forward. Through identifying ongoing professional development needs, this should give you the opportunity to begin your first job with a clear vision of how you want to continue your professional development.

APPLYING FOR JOBS

30

Entering the world of work can be daunting at any age. Finding suitable employment, going through the application process, getting through the interviews, and then starting your first position in the field can be a real challenge.

Upon completion of your final placement, there are several factors to consider in deciding what the right position might be for you.

Client Populations

For some people, their placements may have shown them exactly where their strengths may be, whereas other people complete their field placement feeling uncertain as to where their skills and abilities may be best employed. It is worth spending some time considering options you may not have thought about before, scanning job postings and examining personal strengths to see if a different area of work may fit with your interests and skills. It may also be helpful for you to arrange further shadowing opportunities within different agencies, organizations or institutions towards the end of your placement (if you have time!) in order to gain exposure to other aspects of the field.

Job Security

There is a wealth of benefits and challenges in working within different sectors and settings (see also Chapter 9). In terms of employment, it is worth noting that while no job is secure forever, there are some sectors that provide more security then other sectors. The voluntary sector and its funding can present challenges for some people who value security, although it can offer a wealth of opportunities and provide for lots of diversity of experience. In a world where nothing is stable or secure, how important is a permanent position for you? Some people feel more able to take on a temporary or time-limited contract early on in their career in order to build their confidence and resume, and for some people a temporary position may not be right for them.

Rate of Pay

While we all do this type of work because of a wide range of reasons, the rate of pay and benefits is an important factor for most of us. Some child welfare agencies now offer signing bonuses, as well as other benefits, such as gym memberships, health care benefits, pensions, retention bonuses, and protected caseloads. The pay and benefits of each job are important consideration when you choose which position to apply for.

Staff, Work Teams and Organizational Culture

The role that staff, work teams and the organizational culture in the workplace is important. This can impact your perception of your work environment, whether or not you feel comfortable at work, and whether or not you enjoy your job. Only you know what is right for you in terms of staff, work teams, and organizational culture – some people prefer a lot of desk work and having a busy workload, and some prefer a slower pace within a more reflective environment.

Opportunities for Advancement

Linked to pay and benefits, is the need to consider the opportunities for advancement either upwards or sideways within the agency, organization or institution. Sometimes, at the beginning of your career, opportunities for advancement may be an important factor to consider.

Access to Training and Learning Opportunities

The need for ongoing professional development throughout your career is a crucial consideration for most students entering the field. Training and learning opportunities are important when considering possible employment possibilities. You will also want to evaluate whether the position itself matches the future learning goals and objectives identified at the end of your field placement and program of study.

Orientation

As a student, the need for a comprehensive orientation or induction is obvious, but the same is true for beginning graduates entering the field. When you visit an agency, organization or institution for interview or before accepting a position, it can be a helpful to ask about the orientation process you will receive to ensure it works for you.

Home / Work Balance

Consider the question, do you want to work to live or live to work? Work and life balance is an easy concept to say, but how good are you at achieving this? While dedication is important, we would suggest that nobody can be entirely successful or productive at work if they work till 11 each night and worry about clients on weekends.

Distance

There is value in considering the need to not live in the exact same geographical location where you work, particularly if you work in certain roles. Many SSWs, CYWs, DSWs choose to live a certain distance away from where you work because of personal safety issues and not wanting clients or themselves to feel like they have to constantly interact with one another. It is also important to think about how far you are prepared to travel for work, how you will be getting there, and the cost of travel. Would you move for the right position or experience?

Personal Factors

We all have personal and professional lives, and for many of us, there are important questions which you need to have answered as part of the employment application process, such as whether the employer has policies for employees, family-friendly policies, whether flexible working practices are encouraged or not and child care arrangements.

Looking for Jobs

Not all employment opportunities are advertised in the local paper, but the Internet and employment support services can be key tools for finding the right position for you.

When you see a job advertisement that jumps out, be sure to read it in detail. This sounds obvious, but as an employer it can be really frustrating to receive applications where somebody has thought the job was something totally different from what it actually is. Working with graduates who have misunderstood a job advertisement can be frustrating for employers. If you don't read the job posting and have all of the supporting documents (person specification, job description and any background information on the service and employer), you may be wasting your time and energy!

Job Applications

- Don't submit the same resume and cover letter for each job – it's really obvious when candidates do this. Make your resume and cover letter specific to requirements of the position you are applying for. The human resources department or recruiting manager can only shortlist for interviews based on the criteria outlined in the job posting, so make sure that you state WHY and HOW you meet the requirement for the position.

- What sets you apart from others – Has there been something in your program which you have really enjoyed (e.g.: research, specific areas of interest, or voluntary work)? What makes you the right person for this position?

- Keep Positive - Don't use negative statements on applications. You need to come across as positive with both your cover letter and resume. To give an example of this – some applications ask why you left your previous employer. You may well have left because of a negative experience; however it is best if you can turn this into a positive. For example, if you say you left to broaden your experiences and to develop further skills (or similar) this will sound as though you have a positive rather than negative attitude.

- Read up on the sector and geographical area where you will be working, including the community resources, its strategic priorities and its demographic profile. You may be applying for jobs against twenty other workers all with the same qualification as you, and if you write something which sets you above them and shows the recruiting manager that you really want their job, you are much more likely to get it.

- Describe what you gained from your field placements – This shows that you have thought about the transferability of the skills and experiences you have gained and that you are planning for your future career.

- Give examples – Without going into too much detail, it can be helpful to give specific examples from your field placement to show how you meet the requirements of the position, and how you have applied the knowledge and values you hold. Keep examples brief and obviously consider confidentiality, but it can set you apart from your peers to refer to group work you have done, meetings you have facilitated, or specific pieces of work you are proud of.

- Check it! Again, this may sound obvious, but do not under-estimate the importance of reading through a job posting. Proof read your submission before sending in your application. Use a spelling and grammar check (or a friend) as your written communication skills are important in positions where your assessments and reports will be read by a wide range of audiences.

Your Interviews

- Plan your route beforehand so you know where you are going and how long it takes to get there. Build in some extra travel time in case of traffic too!

- Consideration needs to be made in terms of what to wear to the interview.

- If there is a presentation, practice! Key skills in doing a presentation include maintaining eye contact, smiling, using cards so you have a list of key points to glance at (but don't look down and read word for word as this makes a presentation very dull for the listener!), and use visual aids such as a flipchart sheet if there is no PowerPoint in order to give the interview panel something to look at. Structure is vital – consider why they have written the specific title for the presentation and what they want to know about you and your preparation for this role, and then structure what you say around this.

- In the formal part of an interview take your time and ask the interviewers to repeat any question which you do not understand. For each answer, think about what they are looking for and take your time to add in what would be essential for them to hear from you. The questions are not meant to trick you, but to give you an opportunity to get to know you and make sure you have the knowledge, skills and abilities to be successful in the role. Remember

Top Tips for Interviews
- Be prompt
- Dress smart
- Practice any presentation
- Answer clearly and confidently, avoiding 'yes' or 'no' answers
- Demonstrate your knowledge of the organization
- Be positive
- Maintain eye contact
- Show an interest in the position

interviewers may score your answers so again consider what will set you above others, giving specific examples, and taking a pause at the end of each answer to check that you have covered every key point you want to make.

- Ask questions at the end. If you have a list of two or three questions to ask, it does show that you want the position and you have thought about what it may entail. You may wish to use the checklist above to develop your questions around.

After the Interview

When you are offered a position, think about whether or not you want it? Applying for position is just as much about whether it suits you as whether you suit the employer.

It may be better to turn a job down than take it and leave after three months as this can look bad on you and create an issue for the employer. The field is a small network, so it is important to remember that the reputation you create for yourself, even when you are on short term agency contracts will stay with you throughout your career.

If you are unsure about accepting a job or not, you could ask to visit the agency, organization or institution again so you can meet your potential future colleagues, and assess whether the work teams and the organizational culture will work for you. Don't be afraid to ask questions about workloads as a safe caseload and regular supervision can be important issues for people well into their careers as well as for newly qualified SSW's, CYW's and DSW's.

If you are not offered the job, then feedback is key and you should not be scared to ask for this. The person who has made the decision should be trained in giving specific and constructive feedback, so that you can answer questions in more detail and be successful in the future.

But I Need a Job!

Going for interviews and not getting job offers can be stressful and demoralizing even for the most confident person. Even if you do not get the jobs you want, there are still options, such as volunteer work which can help you broaden your resume, get to know key people in various agencies, organizations and institutions. Networking can give you opportunities which could lead to employment.

SUMMARY

Preparation is the key to finding the right position, doing the best application you can, and being successful during the interview are critical to securing employment in your field. Remember that your work and life balance is important too!

PROFESSIONAL DEVELOMENT

Completing the educational requirements is only the beginning on a continuum of training opportunities in the field. Ongoing professional development training is important to all professionals in the human services field.

All SSW's are required to register with the Ontario College of Social Workers and Social Service Workers if they wish to pursue a career as a Social Service Worker. In order to ensure continued registration, all registered social service workers are required to complete professional development training as part of Continuing Competence Portfolio which has already been discussed. This professional development training may involve attending training, seminars or courses, reading or teaching or other activities that would support the achievement of goals and objectives outlined in the portfolio. A record must be kept of your professional development training and learning in the Continuing Competence Portfolio. CYW's, DSW's and other related human service workers while not regulated currently, would benefit from maintaining a professional development portfolio detailing their continuing competence in the field.

Newly Qualified

The learning and development needs of newly qualified professionals may be different than for those who have been practicing for years. Learning goals and objectives are typically related to their current position.

Continuing Your Learning and Development

While it is not a requirement for qualified workers to engage in a formal program of study as part of registration, each year upon registration Social Service Worker and Social Workers are required to create goals and objectives for further development. Many Social Service Workers transition into the role of Social Work by completing the requirements of a Bachelor of Social Work and a Master's of Social Work. As previously discussed, the level of education and training leads to different designations depending on whether you trained at the college level diploma, bachelor or masters level degree. Similarly, CYWs and DSWs may transition into bachelors of Social Work or related bachelors or masters' level degree.

While there is currently no national requirement for SSW, CYW and DSWs to complete; each province has their own separate regulatory body and typically recognizes the training from one province to the next through the submission of a professional development portfolio.

SUMMARY

Continuing professional development is critical for all professionals working in the human service sector. All registered social workers and social services workers are required to annually complete a Continuing Competence Portfolio as part of their registration each year.

KEY LEARNING POINTS: SECTION H

- Identifying your future learning goals and objectives should be done in partnership with your Field Work Supervisor at the end of your final placement
- Preparation is key to finding the right job
- Continual Professional Development is important for maintaining competency in the field
- Social work has a clearly defined process required in order to maintain registration in Ontario.
- The field of social work has three level of training – the Social Service Worker diploma, the Bachelor of Social Work and the Masters of Social Work.

BIBLIOGRAPHY

Akhurst, J. (2006). Peer Group Supervision as an Adjunct to Individual Supervision: optimizing Learning Processes During Psychologists' Training. *Psychology Teaching Review*, 3-15.

Alfred Kadushin, A., & Harkness, D. (2002). *Supervision in Social Work.* New York: Columbia University Press.

Alle-Corliss, L., & Alle-Corliss, R. (1999). *Advanced Practice in Human Service Agencies: Issues, Trends and Treatment Perspectives.* Belmont: Wadsworth.

Alvarex, A., & Moxley, D. (2004). The Student Portfolio in Social Work Education. *Journal of Teaching in Social Work*, 87-104.

Atherton, S. (2006). *Putting Group Learning into Practice in Social Work Education.* Leeds: Skills for Care in Partnership with the West Midlands Learning Resource Network.

Australian Learning & Teaching Council. (2010). *A Guide to Supervision in Social Work Field Education.* Creative Commons.

Baird, B. (1999). *The Internship, Practicum and Field Placement Handbook: A Guide for the Helping Prfession.* Upper Saddle River, NJ: Prentice Hall.

Barker, R. (1999). *The Social Work Dictionary, 4th Ed.* Washington: NASW Press.

Bogo, M. (2010). *Achieving Competence in Social Work through Field Eduaction.* Toronto: University of Toronto Press.

Bogo, M. (2010). *Achieving Competence in Social Work through Field Eduaction.* Toronto: University of Toronto Press.

Bogo, M., Patterson, J., Tufford, L., & King, R. (2011). Interprofessional Clincal Supervision in Mental Health and Addiction: Toward Identifying Common Elements. *The Clinical Supervisor*, 125.

Bogo, M.; Vayda, E. (1998). *The Practice of Field Instruction in Social Work: Theory and Practice, 2nd Ed.* Toronto: University of Toronto.

Boyd, E., & Fales, A. (1983). Reflecting Learning: Key to Learnign from Experience. *Journal of Humanistic Psychology*, 99-117.

Brown, J., Collins, A., & Duguid, S. (1989). Situated Cognition and the Culture of Learning. *Educational Researcher*, 32-42.

Canadian Association of Social Work Education. (2007). *Accreditation Manual.* Toronto: CASWE.

Carper, B. (1978). Fundamental Patterns of Knowing in Nursing. *Advances in Nursing Sciences*, 13-23.

Carraccio, C; et al. (2002). Shifting Paradigms: From Flexner to Competencies. *Academic Medical*, 361-367.

Chiaferri, R., & Griffin, M. (1997). *Developing Fieldwork Skills: A Guide for Human Services, Counselling, and Social Work Studnets.* Pacific Grove: Brooks/Cole.

Dalhousie University. (n.d.). *Learning Logs.* Retrieved from http://channelcontent.dal.ca/portfolio/r_learnlogs.html

Davys, A., & Biddoe, L. (2000). Supervision of Students: A Map and a Model for the Decade to Come. *Social Work Education*, 437-449.

Doel, M., & Shardlow, S. (1998). *The New Social Work Practice: Exercises and Activities.* Aldershot: Ashgate.

Drolet, J., & Clark, N. A. (2012). *Shifting Sites of Practice field Education in Canada.* Toronto : Pearson Canada Inc.

DSSIG. (2011, 06 06). *Standards of Practice.* Retrieved from Developmental Services Special Interest Group of OADD: http://www.oadd.org/DSSIG_544.html

Felder, R., & Spurlin, J. (2005). A Valaidation Study of the Index of Learning Styles, Applications, Reliability and Validity of the Index of Learning Styles. *International Journal of Engineering Education,* 103-112.

Festinger, L. (1957). *A Theory of Cognitive Dissonance.* Stanford: Stanford University Press.

Fletcher, S. (1992). *Competence Based Assessment Techniques.* London: Kogan Page.

Ford, K., & Jones, A. (1987). *Student Supervision.* London: BASW Macmillan.

Fortune, A., McCarthy, M., & J.Abramson. (2001). Student Learnign Processes in field Education:Relationship of Learnign Activities to Qulaity of field Instruction, Satisfaction and Performatnce Amonf MSW Students. *Journal of Social Work Education,* 111-123.

Furness, S., & Gilligan, P. (2004). Fit for Practice: Issues from Practice Placements, Practice Teaching and the Assessments of Students' Practice. *Social Work Education, 23,* 465-479.

Gibelman & Furman. (2008). *Navigating Human Service Organizations, 2nd Ed.* Chicago: Lyceum Books.

Gibelman, M. (1998). Theory, Practice and Experience in the Purchase of Services. In M. Gibelman, & H. Demone (Eds.), *The Privatization of Human Service:Policy and Practical Issues* (Vol. 1, pp. 1-51). New York: Springer.

Harkness, D., & Poertner, J. (1989). Research and Social Work Supervision: A Conceptual Review. *Social Work, 34(2),* 115-119.

Holland, T. (1995). Organizations:Context For Social Service Delivery. In R. Edwards, *Encyclopedia of Social Work, 19th Ed.* (p. 1787). Washington: NASW Press.

Honey, P., & Mumford, A. (1982). *Manual of Learning Styles.* Peter Honey Publications.

Honey, P., & Mumford, A. (1986). *Using Your Learning Styles.* Peter Honey Publication.

Horejsi, C., & Garthwait, C. (2004). *The Social Work PracticumL A Guide and Workbook for Students.* Boston: Allyn & Bacon.

Houghton, W. (2004). *The higher Education Academy.* Retrieved from Engineering Subject Centre: http://www.engsc.ac.uk/learning-and-teaching-theory-guide/deep-and-surface-approaches-learning

HRDC. (2011, November 14th). *www.hrsdc.gc.ca.* Retrieved from Human Resources and Skills Development Canada: http://www5.hrsdc.gc.ca/noc/english/noc/2006/QuickSearch.aspx?val65=4212

Johns, C. (1995). The Value of Reflective Practice for Nursing. *Journal of Nursing,* 23-30.

Kadushin, A. (1985). *Supervision in Social Work, 2nd Ed.* New York: Columbia University Press.

Kadushin, A. (1992). *Supervision in Social Work, 3rd Ed.* New York: Columbia University Press.

Kadushin, A., & Harkness, D. (2002). *Supervision in Social Work, 4th ed.* New York: Columbia Unversity Press.

King, J. (2007). *Recieving Feedback Gracefully is a Critical Career Skill.* Retrieved from The Sideroad: http://www.sideroad.com/Career_Advice/receiving-feedback.html

Kolb, D. (1984). *Experiential Learning: Experience as the Source of Learning and Development.* New Jersey: Prentice Hall.

Lave, J., & Wenger, E. (1990). *Situated Learning: Legitimate Peripheral Participation.* Cambridge: Cambridge University Press.

Linn, J. (2000). *Jane Adams. A Biography.* Urbana: university of Illinois Press.

Maclean, S. (2007). *Developing Partnership Working in Social Work Education: Where are we now?* West Midlands: Skills for Care.

Marsh, S., Cooper, K., Jordon, G., Merrett, S., Scammel, J., & Clark, V. (2005). *Making Practice Learning Work.* Retrieved from Assessment of Students in Health and Social Care: Managing Failing Students in Practice: http://www.science.ulster.ac.uk/nursing/mentorship/docs/learning/Failing_students_final_version_22%20Nov.pdf

Marton, F., & Saljo, R. (1976). On Qualitative Differences in Learning: Outcome and Process. *British Journal of Educational Psychology*, 4-11.

MCSS. (1998). *Social Work and Social Service Work Act.* Toronto: Ministry of Community and Social Services.

Moore, P. (2001). Critical Components of an Anti-oppressive Framework. *Journal of Child and Youth Care*, 25-32.

Morrison, T. (2005). *Staff Supervision in Social Care: Making a Real Difference for Staff and Service Users.* Brighton: Pavilion Publishing Ltd.

MTCU. (2012). *Developmental Services Program Standards.* Toronto: Queens Printer.

MTCU. (2007). *Social Service Worker Program Standard.* Toronto: Ministry of Training, Colleges and Universities.

MTCU. (2007). *Social Service Worker Program Standards.* Toronto: Queens Printer.

Mullins, L. (2005). *Managment and Organizational Behaviour, 7th Ed.* London: Kogan Page.

Myers Kiser, P. (2008). *the Human Service Internship: Getting the Most from Your Experience, 2nd Ed.* Belmont, CA: Brooks/Cole.

NOPT. (2004). *Code of Practice for Practice Teachers.* Manchester: National Organization of Practice Teaching.

NUPGE. (2011, 11, 03). *National Union of Public and General Employees.* Retrieved from National Union: http://www.nupge.ca/content/4597/forth-year-community-social-service-worker-appreciation-day

OACYC. (2010). *Code of Ethics.* Retrieved from Ontario Association of Child and Youth Counsellors: http://www.oacyc.org/index.php?page=14

OCSWSSW. (2008). *Code of Ethics and Standards of Practice Handbook, 2nd Ed,.* Toronto: Ontario College of Social Work and Social Service Workers.

OCSWSSW. (2009). *Continuing Competence Program Instruction Guide.* Toronto: Ontario Colllege of Social Work and Social Service Workers.

OCSWSSW. (2008). *Position Paper on Scope of Practice.* Toronto: Ontario College of Social Work and Social Service Worker.

OCSWSSW. (2008). *Position Paper on the Scope of Practice.* Toronto: Ontario College of Social Work and Social Service Worker.

OCSWSSW. (2012). *Practice Notes: Supervision: At the Core of Competence and Ethical Practice.* Toronto: Ontario College of Social Work and Social Service Workers.

Ontario Human Rights Commission. (2002). *Policy and Guidelines on Disability and the Duty to Accomodate.* Toronto: OHRC.

Ontario Human Rights Commission. (2002). *The Opportuntiy to Succeed: Achieving Barrier-Free Education for Students with Disabiliites.* Toronto: OHRC.

Ontario Ministry of Citizenship and Immigration. (2008, March). *Career Map.* Retrieved from Ontario Immigration: http://www.ontarioimmigration.ca/en/working/OI_HOW_WORK_SOCWORKER_CM.html

Ontario Public Service. (2005). *Reviewing The Accessibility For Ontarians With Disabilities Act.* Retrieved from Ontario Public Service: http://news.ontario.ca/mcss/en/2009/06/reviewing-the-accessibility-for-ontarians-with-disabilities-act.html

Parker, J. (2004). *Effective Practice Learning in Social Work.* Exeter: Learning Matters Ltd.

Phillips, R. (1998). Disabled Students: Barriers to Practice Learning. *Journal of Practice Teaching,* 13-23.

Ranson, C. (2011, 06). *Educational Blogging to Promote Reflective Clinical Practice.* Retrieved from ETEC 510: Design Wiki: http://sites.wiki.ubc.ca/etec510/Educational_Blogging_to_Promote_Reflective_Clinical_Practice#Reflective_Practice

Rich, P. (2009). *Giving and Receiving Feedback.* Retrieved from Self Help Magazine: http://www.selfhelpmagazine.com/article/giving-feedback

RMIT. (2006). *Study and Learning Centre.* Retrieved from RMIT University: http://www.dlsweb.rmit.edu.au/lsu/content/2_AssessmentTasks/assess_tuts/reflective%20journal_LL/index.html

RNAO. (2012). *Registered Nurses Association of Ontario.* Retrieved from Self Directed Learning: http://www.rnao.org/Self_Directed_Learning/sect3Lesson5Part1.htm

Rose, S., & Black, B. (1985). *Advocacy and empowerment:Mental Health Care in the Community.* Boston: Routledge and Kegan Paul.

Saunders, R. (2004, January). *Passion and Commitment Under Stress:Human Resouce Issues in Canada's Non-Profit Sector.* Retrieved from Canadian Policy Reseach Networks Inc.: http://www.cpm.org/en/doc.cfm?doc+504#

Schatz, M. (2004). Using Portfolios: Integrating Learning and Promoting for Social Work Students. *Advances in Social Work,* 105-123.

Schatz, M., & Simon, S. (1999). The Portfolio Approach for Generalist Social Work Practice: A Successful Tool for Students in Field Education. *Journal of Baccalaureate Social Work,* 99-107.

Schön, D. (1987). *Educating the Reflective Practitioner.* San Franscisco: Jossey Bass.

Sinclair, C. (2006). *Keeping A Reflective Journal: Reflections of a Mature Student.* Paisley: University of Paisley.

Smith, L. H. (2006). *5 Basic Skills To Improve Performance in Work, Sport, or Life.* Retrieved from Personal Best Consulting: http://www.personalbestconsulting.com/article_47.html

SWAP. (2007). *Social Policy and Social Work Subject Centre.* Southampton: Higher Education Academy.

SWAP. (2007). *The Social Work Degree: Preparing to Succeed.* Southampton: High Education Academy.

Thomlinson, B., Rogers, G., Collins, D., & Ginnell, R. (1996). *The Social Work Practicum: An Access Guide.* Itasca: Peacock.

Turner, F. J. (2002). *Social Work Practice, A Canadian Perspective, 2nd. Ed.* Toronto: Prentice Hall.

Webb, N. (1988). The Role of the Field Instructor in the Socialization of Students. *Social Casework 69,* 35-40.

Williams, S., & Rutter, L. (2007). *Enabling and Assessing Work Based Learning for Social Work: Supporting the Development of Professional Practice.* Birmingham: Learn to Care.

Wilson, S. (1981). *Field Instructor:Techniques for Supervisors.* New York: Free Press.

Wray, J., Fell, B., Stanley, J., Manthorpe, J., & Coyne, E. (2005). *The PEdDS Project: Disabled Social Work Studnets And Placements.* Hull: University of Hull.